# Gath                                           e

# AMISH TABLE

D1709639

# Gather around the AMISH TABLE

### TREASURED RECIPES AND STORIES FROM PLAIN COMMUNITIES

## Lucy Leid

**Herald Press**

Harrisonburg, Virginia
Kitchener, Ontario

Library of Congress Cataloging-in-Publication Data
Gather around the Amish table : treasured recipes and stories from plain communities /
Lucy Leid, compiler.
    pages cm
 Includes bibliographical references.
  ISBN 978-0-8361-9910-9 (pbk. : alk. paper)  1.  Amish cooking.  2.  Mennonite cooking.
3.  Amish Country (Pa.)--Social life and customs.  I. Leid, Lucy, 1953-
  TX721.G38 2015
  641.5'66--dc23
                                                                          2014043025

GATHER AROUND THE AMISH TABLE
© 2015 by Herald Press, Harrisonburg, Virginia 22802
    Released simultaneously in Canada by Herald Press,
    Kitchener, Ontario N2G 3R1. All rights reserved.
Library of Congress Control Number: 2014043025
International Standard Book Number: 978-0-8361-9910-9
Printed in United States of America
Cover and interior design by Merrill Miller
Cover photo by Melissa Engle

Food photography by Melissa Engle. Food styling by Cherise Harper.
Additional photos by Thinkstock except for the following: Cindy Cornett Seigle/Creative
Commons: 116–17, 234, 268–69. Merrill Miller: 61.

An earlier version of this book was published as *Countryside Cooking & Chatting* (Herald
Press, 2006).

To order or request information, please call 1-800-245-7894 or visit www.heraldpress.com.

19 18 17 16 15        10 9 8 7 6 5 4 3 2 1

# Contents

# Introduction

This book in your hands is a charming glimpse into the kitchens and lives of horse-and-buggy people. With their stories and recipes, they invite us to fellowship around their tables. The cooks admit their mistakes and their lessons and share their jokes.

The recipes run the gamut from good old country cooking in staggering amounts (Clara's Sugar Cookies, Midwestern Casserole) to a more modern awareness of whole grains and less sugar (100% Whole Wheat Bread, Three-Bean Salad). Since the recipes came straight from the recipe boxes in response to Lucy's invitation, we standardized and clarified the recipes. Some recipes instructed cooks to "mix and bake until done" or "add enough flour;" we tested those recipes and filled in the temperatures, amounts, and methods for those of us who are less experienced in the kitchen.

We have preserved the tone and cadence of the contributors' words, however, so you can feel the warmth of the generous natures behind this cookbook. In true plain fashion, none of the cooks wanted to be named in this cookbook. Lucy herself does not care if her name is on the project or not. She is more interested in the stories: the mother who sent in the directions for Homemade Baby Wipes, how a Popover Pizza was first named "flop-over pizza" by the contributor's brothers, why a mother would fry eight dozen Overnight Doughnuts by seven a.m. . . .

Enjoy the stories and the good food. May God bless your fellowship around your own table with the ones you love.

*The Editors*

# Compiler's Note

I think I have been reading *Die Botschaft* for about thirty years. It comes weekly from Millersburg, Pennsylvania, about forty sheets of newsprint full of news from the letters that the scribes sent in. The scribes are the reporters in the various Amish and horse-and-buggy Mennonite communities around the country; I don't think anyone with a car is allowed to be a scribe.

The scribes report on the general news of the neighborhood, usually starting out with "Greetings from Indiana" or "Hello to all from Pennsylvania!" They write about where church was held, how the crops are doing, the weather, who's visiting, who's home from the hospital, and such. Then there are births, deaths, prayer requests, and classified ads.

At the end is *Ivverich und Ender* ("what's left over, the ends"), which has address requests, recipes, thank yous, and other miscellaneous things. I got the idea for this cookbook from seeing other people's ads in *Ivverich und Ender*. I asked people to send me their "tried-and-true" recipes along with some chatting, a story about the recipe or food. There are so many cookbooks around, but I wanted a cookbook with stories in it, too, with the kinds of sharing I enjoy from *Die Botschaft*. Some of the stories are composites that I and my helpers drew up from several anecdotes on a similar theme.

I'm really not a fancy cook. I don't make lots of baked good or desserts. My specialty is soups and stews. I like to keep cooked rice and barley on hand to add to them. We eat lots of garden vegetables, but I really don't use recipes for anything I cook unless company is coming. I hope you find some good recipes in this collection, and I hope you enjoy the encouragement and laughs from the stories. It's one of the blessings of life to share ourselves with each other.

*Lucy Leid*
*Hinkletown, Pennsylvania, 2015*

# Notes on Ingredients and Terms

**Therm-flo** and **Clear Jel** are corn-based thickeners. They give a nicer texture than cornstarch and won't turn cloudy. There are two kinds of Clear Jel: instant and cook-type. Instant Clear Jel does not need heat to thicken, but cook-type must be cooked with the liquid first in order to thicken. Sure-Jell cannot be substituted for Clear Jel. (Sure-Jell is a fruit pectin for homemade jams and jellies.)

**Dinner** refers to the noon meal, **supper** to the evening meal.

**Divided** means that the amount is used in portions as indicated in the recipe directions.

**Karo** is corn syrup.

**Molasses** refers to mild, light molasses or baking molasses, not black-strap molasses. Golden Barrel is one brand.

**Confectioners' sugar** is also known as powdered sugar, 10x sugar, and icing sugar.

**Occident flour** is creamy-colored hard wheat flour, excellent for yeasted baked goods. Substitute unbleached bread flour or unbleached all-purpose flour, although the results may be slightly different.

Breakfast

# Alma's Breakfast Casserole

**Serves 6–8**

## INGREDIENTS

**2**  cups bread cubes

**½**  pound bacon, diced and fried

**¼**  cup celery, diced

**¼**  cup red bell pepper, diced

**8**  eggs

**2**  cups milk

**1**  teaspoon salt

paprika

## Note

Ham or cooked chicken can be substituted for bacon.

## INSTRUCTIONS

Cover the bottom of greased 9 x 13-inch pan with bread cubes. Sprinkle bacon on top. Sprinkle celery and pepper over top of the bacon. Beat together eggs, milk, and salt. Pour over bread. Sprinkle with paprika. Bake at 350° for 45 minutes, or until set.

## Lucy's Kitchen Tip

To get rid of flies at the attic windows, set a small tin of kerosene on the windowsill. For some reason, the flies just tumble in. For fruit flies in the kitchen, set out a small dish of vinegar with a few drops of dishwashing soap in it.

# Favorite Breakfast Casserole

**Makes 1 (9 x 13-inch) pan**

Greetings from Indiana! We have a family of five girls and four boys, so there's always plenty of cooking to do. We have several hours of choring before breakfast, and so it takes more than cold cereal at that meal. Breakfast casseroles are handy because they can be prepared the evening before and popped into the oven at the proper time.

I remember one time our two little girls, ages seven and eight, decided to make a breakfast casserole all by themselves, to surprise me. They didn't follow a recipe, just stirred in what they had watched me putting in: eggs, milk, crumbled bread, ham slices, etc. It turned out surprisingly well, if you didn't mind a few eggshells and lack of salt and pepper. I added the cheese on top, and they were on cloud nine about their accomplishment!

## INGREDIENTS

- **6** eggs, beaten
- **2** cups milk
- **6** slices bread, cubed
- **1** teaspoon salt
- **⅛** teaspoon pepper
- **1** teaspoon dry mustard
- **1** pound sausage, fried and drained, or chopped ham
- **1** cup cheddar cheese, shredded
- **1** tablespoon onion, minced

## INSTRUCTIONS

Mix everything together and refrigerate overnight. Bake, uncovered, in a 9 x 13-inch pan the next morning at 350° for 45–60 minutes, until set in the middle.

# Country Breakfast

**Makes 1 (9 x 13-inch) pan**

## INGREDIENTS

**14** slices bread, cubed

**2½** cups ham, cubed

**16** ounces cheddar cheese, shredded

**16** ounces mozzarella cheese, shredded

**6** eggs

**3** cups milk

*Topping*

**3** cups cornflakes or Ritz crackers, crushed

**½** cup butter, melted

## INSTRUCTIONS

Grease a 9 x 13-inch pan and layer half of bread, ham, and cheese. Repeat layers. Beat eggs. Add milk and beat again. Pour egg mixture over layers. Refrigerate overnight. Just before baking, sprinkle with topping. Cover loosely and bake at 375° for 45 minutes.

# Layered Omelet Bake

**Serves 8**

Our Jersey cow is tame and easy to milk, but she has one undesirable trait: finding weak spots in the fence that we didn't know existed and slipping through into the neighbor's field. Naturally, the neighbors aren't very happy about it, and neither are we. I often wonder why she can't be more contented in our lush, green, buttercup-dotted meadow.

One evening she didn't come up to be milked, and I went on a search for her. I found her solidly wedged in between two trees that grew close together, unable to go forward or backward. With the help of a chain saw, Dad got her loose. I hope she has learned her lesson—that sticking her nose where it doesn't belong isn't wise—and won't make any more trouble.

We talked about selling her and buying our milk at the neighbor's dairy, but I know I'd miss the extra milk for butter, cheese, puddings, and ice cream.

## INGREDIENTS

- **16** slices bread, buttered
- **8** slices cheese
- **½** pound shaved ham
- **8** slices bacon, fried and crumbled
- **6** eggs
- **3** cups milk
- **½** teaspoon dry mustard
- **½** teaspoon salt
- **1** cup cornflakes, crushed
- **½** cup margarine or butter, melted

## INSTRUCTIONS

Make 8 sandwiches using bread, cheese, ham, and bacon. Put in a greased 9 x 13-inch pan. Mix eggs, milk, mustard, and salt, and pour over sandwiches. Refrigerate overnight. In the morning, mix cornflakes and margarine and sprinkle on top. Bake at 350° for 1 hour.

## Special Occasion Eggs

**Serves 6**

### INGREDIENTS

**2** tablespoons margarine

**2** cups cheese, divided

**12** eggs

  chipped ham, bacon, bacon bits, or sausage

### INSTRUCTIONS

Grease a 9 x 13-inch pan with margarine. Sprinkle with 1 cup shredded cheese. Crack eggs and space them out on top of cheese. Poke egg yolks but don't stir. Sprinkle with salt and pepper. Choose one or two meats and spread on top of eggs. Sprinkle with 1 cup cheese. Bake at 350° for 30 minutes.

## Gourmet Eggs

**Serves 4**

### INGREDIENTS

**6** eggs

**2** tablespoons cream

¼ teaspoon salt

  dash pepper

  seasoned salt, optional

**3** slices bread

**2** tablespoons butter, melted

  cheese, sliced or grated

### INSTRUCTIONS

Whip eggs, cream, salt, pepper, and optional seasoned salt in the blender. Crumble bread into shallow baking dish. Mix the melted butter with the crumbs, which also butters the dish. Pour egg mixture over buttered crumbs. Bake at 350° for 10 minutes, or until firm. Top with cheese slices or grated cheese. Return to oven until cheese is melted.

# Peanut Butter Granola

**Makes about 12 cups**

## INGREDIENTS

- **1** cup honey
- **½** cup vegetable oil
- **1½** cup peanut butter
- **1** teaspoon vanilla
- **8** cups quick oats
- **1** cup grated coconut
- **1** cup wheat germ
- **1** cup brown sugar
- **½** teaspoon cinnamon
- **½** teaspoon salt

## INSTRUCTIONS

Mix wet ingredients until smooth. Combine with dry ingredients until coated. Spread on rimmed baking sheets. Bake at 250° until slightly browned, about 1 hour, stirring every 15 minutes or so.

# Pecan Granola

**Makes about 10 cups**

## INGREDIENTS

- **6** cups rolled or quick oats
- **1½** cup brown sugar
- **2** cups grated coconut
- **1** cup pecans, chopped
- **½** cup wheat germ
- **½** cup butter, melted

## INSTRUCTIONS

Mix well. Spread onto baking sheets. Toast to golden brown in slow oven (about 300°), stirring occasionally, for about 45 minutes. May add ½ cup raisins after the granola is cool.

# Mary's Granola

**Makes about 25 cups**

*I got this recipe out of a circle letter the first year we were married, which is twenty-three years ago now, and we have used it almost every summer. At first, I used only rolled oats, and now in thinking back, it was very chewy. However, my sister-in-law informed me that quick oats could also be used. I've decided we like it best with mixed oats.*

*It's a real favorite with our family, although they also like cornflakes. As for me, I think cornflakes can get sort of soggy, so I still stick to my granola!*

## INGREDIENTS

**12** cups quick oats

**8** cups rolled oats

**2** cups brown sugar

**4** cups grated coconut

**2** teaspoons salt

**1** teaspoon cinnamon

**8** teaspoons vanilla

**2** cups Karo or maple syrup

## INSTRUCTIONS

Mix all ingredients. Spread onto baking sheets. Toast to a nice brown at 300°, stirring occasionally, for up to 1 hour. Add raisins and sunflower seeds after the granola is cool.

# Nut Caramel Oatmeal

**Serves 4**

## INGREDIENTS

**2** eggs, beaten

**3½** cups milk

**½** teaspoon salt

**1** cup brown sugar

**2** cups quick oats

**¼** cup margarine

**¼** cup nuts

## INSTRUCTIONS

Mix eggs, milk, salt, and sugar in a saucepan. Cook and stir until bubbly. Stir in oats and cook until bubbly again. Add margarine and nuts. Cover and remove from heat. Let stand 5 minutes. Stir and serve with milk.

# Cinnamon Baked Oatmeal

**Serves 4–6**

*We like oatmeal for breakfast every morning, usually just cooked, with a handful of raisins thrown in. For special occasions and for variety, we sometimes make this baked oatmeal.*

*One day last spring, I took a pan of it out of the oven and set it on the windowsill with the window pushed up so it could cool off before the rest came in from doing barn chores. I set the table and then went out to the milk house for a pitcher of milk. While I was out, one of the boys asked for a bit of help with a calf he was feeding, which took some time.*

*By the time we came in, later than usual, to eat breakfast, mischief had been done. Our rascally pet crow flew noisily away from the window—he knew he was guilty! He had pecked and scratched at the baked oatmeal and crumbs were all over. No one felt like eating any of it after his feet and beak had been in it. If we wouldn't all be so attached to him, he wouldn't get away with such things.*

## INGREDIENTS

- **½** cup butter, melted
- **1** cup brown sugar
- **2** eggs
- **½** teaspoon cinnamon
- **3** cups quick oats
- **2** teaspoons baking powder
- **1** teaspoon salt
- **1** cup milk

## INSTRUCTIONS

Cream together butter, brown sugar, and eggs. Add the rest of ingredients to creamed mixture. Bake in 9 x 9-inch pan at 350° for 20–30 minutes. Can be mixed the night before.

# Apple Raisin Bake

**Serves 2–4**

## INGREDIENTS

**1½** cup water

**½** cup maple or pancake syrup

**1½** cup oats (can use quick or rolled)

**½** teaspoon salt (scant)

**¼** cup honey

**½** teaspoon cinnamon

**2** medium apples, pared, thinly sliced

**½** cup raisins

## INSTRUCTIONS

Bring water to a boil in a medium saucepan with the syrup. Stir in oatmeal and salt. Cook 1 minute. (If using rolled oats, cook 5 minutes.) Stir in honey and cinnamon. Remove from heat and put half the oatmeal into a 1½-quart casserole dish; top with half the apples and half the raisins. Add remaining oatmeal, then top with the rest of the apples and raisins. Cover. Bake at 350° for 20–25 minutes. Serve with milk.

# Corn Pone

**Serves 4–6**

*I remember eating this "cake" for breakfast as a little girl with milk and fruit. It's also called Johnny cake, although I read somewhere once that the proper name is Journey cake.*

*Our favorite fruit topping was, and still is, applesauce. We considered it as a kind of cereal at home, since we ate it for breakfast. I'm still using the same recipe my mother did and will pass it on to my daughters, although my family now eats it as a dessert with honey on it.*

## INGREDIENTS

**1** cup cornmeal

**1** cup flour

**½** teaspoon salt

**4** teaspoons baking powder

**1** egg, beaten

**1** cup milk

**¼** cup shortening or oil

## INSTRUCTIONS

Mix dry ingredients in a bowl. Make a well and add egg, milk, and shortening or oil. Mix just until combined. Pour into greased 9 x 9-inch pan. Bake at 350° for 30–35 minutes.

## Note

To use sour milk or buttermilk, reduce the baking powder to 1 tablespoon and add 1 teaspoon baking soda.

# Whole Wheat Pancakes

**Serves 4**

### INGREDIENTS

**1½** cup whole wheat flour

**½** teaspoon baking powder

**1** teaspoon baking soda

**¾** teaspoon salt

**2** eggs, beaten

**1½** cup buttermilk or sour milk

**4** tablespoons vegetable oil

### INSTRUCTIONS

Thoroughly mix dry ingredients. Separately, combine eggs, buttermilk, and oil. Add to dry ingredients and mix just until smooth. Fry on hot, lightly greased griddle.

# Apple Pancakes

**Serves 4–6**

### INGREDIENTS

**2** cups flour

**2** tablespoons sugar

**1** tablespoon baking powder

**1** teaspoon salt

**½** teaspoon cinnamon

**1** egg

**1¼** cup milk

**2** tablespoons vegetable oil

**¼** cup apples, finely diced

### INSTRUCTIONS

Mix dry ingredients. Add wet ingredients and apples just until mixed. Fry on hot, lightly greased griddle.

# Linda's Pancakes

**Serves 4**

*Once when I was making pancakes, I couldn't find the bottle of vegetable oil. I pulled the step stool to the pantry shelf and was moving things around, when suddenly a mouse popped out and nearly ran into my face! It surprised and scared me so much that I made a sound like a war whoop, which my brothers heard out in the barn! Now when I need something from the pantry shelf, I send my younger sister, who isn't at all scared of mice.*

## INGREDIENTS

- **1** egg
- **1** cup all-purpose flour
- **¾** cup milk
- **1** tablespoon sugar
- **2** tablespoons shortening, melted, or vegetable oil
- **1** tablespoon baking powder
- **½** teaspoon salt

## INSTRUCTIONS

Beat egg with hand beater or whisk until foamy. Stir in remaining ingredients just until smooth. For thinner pancakes, stir in additional ¼ cup milk. Grease heated griddle. To test griddle, sprinkle with a few drops of water. If bubbles skitter around, heat is just right. For each pancake, pour about 3 tablespoons batter from tip of spoon or pitcher onto hot griddle. Cook until puffed and dry around edges. Turn and cook other side until golden brown.

# Mom's Waffles

**Serves 4**

This recipe was handed down to me by my mother. After twenty-four years of use, my recipe card is worn and yellow. It's been a favorite of our family, mostly served for Sunday brunch. We like waffles with butter, jelly, honey, or maple syrup, or topped with chicken and gravy or ham and gravy. We also all like waffles for dessert, topped with vanilla ice cream and strawberry jam.

Last time we had waffles, our twenty-three-year-old son suggested we try warm apple pie filling with whipped cream on top, an idea he got from a restaurant. Delicious!

## INGREDIENTS

- **1¾** cup all-purpose flour
- **2** teaspoons baking powder
- **1** teaspoon baking soda
- **½** teaspoon salt
- **2** teaspoons sugar
- **3** eggs, well beaten
- **1½** cup buttermilk
- **½** cup margarine, melted

## INSTRUCTIONS

Mix dry ingredients. Separately, mix eggs and buttermilk. Add to dry ingredients. Add melted margarine and stir lightly. Bake in waffle pan according to manufacturer's directions.

# Cornmeal Mush

**Serves 6**

Corn husking time, with its bantering and visiting and friendly competition, is here again, only we don't do it by hand anymore. I've always thought that it is such a nice time of year, when most of the cornfields are bare again and only the corn stubbles remain. Now we can see the neighboring farms again and also the creek valley. I like working in the fields when the heat of the summer is past and a person has more energy.

When the weather gets cool, we start to cook cornmeal mush again regularly, and we always have fried mush for breakfast over the winter. It's an economical dish and probably healthier fare than most other recipes. We like it with eggs and homemade ketchup, but Grandpa likes to eat his topped with molasses. Once we had out-of-state guests here for breakfast, and they poured milk over it and ate it with peach slices.

## INGREDIENTS

**3** cups water

**1** cup cornmeal

**1** teaspoon salt

**1** cup milk

## INSTRUCTIONS

Bring water to a boil. Separately, stir together cornmeal, salt, and milk. Add slowly to the boiling water, stirring. Stir until it has reached the boiling point, then stir occasionally. Cook for 15–20 minutes over low heat, then pour into a deep baking dish. Cool. Slice and fry.

### Note

To clean the mush kettle after the mush has been poured out, put a cup or two of water into the kettle. Add 1 teaspoon baking soda. Cover, then bring to the boiling point. Set kettle aside, but keep covered until dishwashing time.

### Lucy's Kitchen Tip

To roast corn for cornmeal, dry nice ears of corn in a slow, open-door oven for several days, or until the corn shells easily. Shell, then grind the kernels into meal. Put it in an oblong pan and bake at 275° for several hours for a more toasted flavor. Stir occasionally. When cool, place in a tight container.

# Flavored Yogurt

**Makes 1 gallon**

*I find this an easy and good yogurt recipe. The first couple times I tried to make yogurt, it was a flop and just stayed runny like sour milk. So I used it for making whoopie pies, and they turned out real good.*

*I got this recipe from my sister-in-law who lives in Indiana. We haven't yet seen where they have lived for almost five years, but I can use her recipe and think of them.*

*We have a dairy farm with sixty cows, so there is always plenty of milk around.*

### INGREDIENTS

**1** gallon milk
⅓ cup cold water
**1½** tablespoon unflavored gelatin
¾ cup sugar
  pinch salt
**1** teaspoon vanilla
**5** tablespoons flavored gelatin
½ cup plain yogurt

### INSTRUCTIONS

Put milk on low heat for 1 hour, or until it reaches 180°. Soak unflavored gelatin in ⅓ cup cold water. Add to warm milk along with sugar, salt, vanilla, and flavored gelatin. Let stand 1 hour, then add the plain yogurt. Put in jars. Keep warm in oven with pilot light on overnight or 8 hours until gelled.

# Sylvia's Favorite Yogurt

**Makes ½ gallon**

*We used to buy our yogurt, but now since we have this recipe, we make our own, and all of us like it much better. Not to mention the money you save, especially if you live on a dairy farm.*

### INGREDIENTS

**2** quarts milk
**4** teaspoons unflavored gelatin
¼ cup cold water
½ cup sugar
½ cup plain yogurt

### INSTRUCTIONS

Heat milk in saucepan to 190°. Let cool to 130°. Meanwhile, soak gelatin in cold water; add to the 130° milk. Mix sugar and yogurt; also add to milk, mixing well. Put mixture in jars. Cover with lids but not rings so the jars are covered loosely. Put in gas oven with pilot light on for 8 hours until firm.

### Note

If you have no pilot light in your oven, put a lamp with a 100-watt bulb in the oven, which works just as well.

# Breads & Spreads

# 100% Whole Wheat Bread

**Makes 4 loaves**

*This is our favorite bread recipe. I make it weekly for our family of four, sometimes twice a week. We use it for toast, sandwiches, and jelly bread. The only time I get flops is when I let the yeast rise too long while it is dissolving—then at the last rising the loaves don't rise much anymore. Since I've been making this bread, my husband doesn't care for white bread anymore, or even the store-bought brown bread.*

## INGREDIENTS

- ⅔ cup honey
- 4½ cups warm water
- 1 tablespoon salt
- 2 tablespoons active dry yeast
- 3 eggs, beaten
- 12–13 cups finely ground whole wheat flour, divided
- 3 tablespoons wheat germ

## INSTRUCTIONS

Mix together honey, water, salt, and yeast. Leave undisturbed until yeast dissolves, about 10 minutes. Beat in eggs and 2 cups flour. Allow to rest, covered, for 30–60 minutes, until bubbly. Stir in enough flour to make a soft, workable dough. Knead in wheat germ. Knead well and let rise twice in bowl. Shape into 4 loaves and place in greased 8-inch loaf pans. Let rise again until not quite doubled. Bake at 350° for 30–40 minutes.

## Note

I sometimes keep a portion of the dough to make breadsticks, letting dough rise once. Flatten dough with rolling pin to about ½ inch. Cut into 1-inch strips and put on cookie sheets. Let rise a little. Bake until golden brown, then dip in melted butter and sprinkle with garlic powder and Italian herb seasoning. Serve with pizza sauce for dipping. Delicious!

# Sarah's Wheat Bread

**Makes 4 loaves**

*These are our favorite bread recipes, the ones we always use. I'll always remember the time I had such a bad scare while I was making this bread. Our little boy was fifteen months old and loved to spend time outdoors. I constantly went to the window to check on him as he played in the sandbox. I had often hinted to my husband that we needed a fence around the yard, but nothing had come of it. I was thinking about this as I kneaded the bread dough. As I often did, I prayed for each member of the family with each punch, and tried to knead "love" into the dough.*

*All at once I realized that it was high time to check on my little boy. My heart sank as I saw him trotting out in the field, headed straight for the pond. I ran so hard! I scooped him up in my arms gratefully with a prayer of thanks. The very next day my husband started digging holes for the fence posts.*

## INGREDIENTS

½ cup sugar

1½ cup warm milk

1½ cup warm potato water (heat to boiling first and allow to cool until warm)

1½ tablespoon active dry yeast

2 cups whole wheat flour

½ cup vegetable oil

1 tablespoon salt

5½ cups bread flour (approximately)

## INSTRUCTIONS

Stir sugar in milk and water. Add yeast and whole wheat flour. Stir well or beat with eggbeater. Let stand until it starts to rise a little, about 20 minutes. Add oil, salt, and rest of flour gradually until a soft dough forms. Knead about 10 minutes. Allow to rise in bowl, covered with dish towel, until double. Form medium-sized loaves and allow to rise again in greased loaf pans, until nearly double. Bake at 350° for 30 minutes.

## Lucy's Kitchen Tip

When making bread or rolls, always have the flour at room temperature before mixing. This encourages the dough to rise nicely.

# Molasses Whole Wheat Bread

**Makes 3 loaves**

*One day a salesman came to make supper for us to demonstrate waterless cooking in the cookware he was selling. He said he usually doesn't stay to eat with the family, but since I was baking this "almost sugar-free" whole wheat bread and he wanted to taste it, he asked to stay. He really liked it, and to my surprise, even asked for the recipe.*

### INGREDIENTS

- **1⅓** cup milk
- **4** tablespoons butter
- **1** tablespoon powdered lecithin
- **1** cup warm water
- **1** heaping tablespoon active dry yeast
- **1** teaspoon sugar
- **1** egg, beaten
- **1** heaping teaspoon salt
- **2** tablespoons honey
- **2** tablespoons blackstrap molasses
- **3½** cups whole wheat flour
- **5½** cups occident bread flour, divided

### INSTRUCTIONS

Heat milk to steaming and add butter and lecithin. Set aside to cool to lukewarm. In a small bowl, dissolve yeast and sugar in warm water. In another bowl, combine egg, salt, honey, and molasses. Add lukewarm milk mixture and then yeast mixture. Then add whole wheat flour. Mix until lumps are gone. Add 1½ cup occident flour. Continue stirring and adding flour until dough isn't sticky, mixing with hands toward the end. Knead. Allow to rise in greased bread bowl, covered with towel. Form into loaves and place in greased loaf pans. Allow to rise again. Bake at 350° for 30 minutes.

### Note

May substitute another egg for the lecithin.

# White Bread

**Makes 6 loaves**

*This is a recipe that my mother-in-law gave to me when we were just married. It is a good recipe to get girls started on bread making and most always gets nice and light.*

*When we were planning to go on a trip and I needed more bread for the chore boys, my husband offered to work the bread dough for me. I had mixed in everything except the flour, so I instructed him to work in fourteen cups of flour. I then left the kitchen to put the little ones in for their naps.*

*Later as I worked down the bread dough, I was puzzled by the texture. My husband remarked, "You women sure work hard to get flour in your bread dough. I just couldn't get fourteen cups in!" Thinking the 2-cup measuring cup was only 1 cup, he had put almost twenty-eight cups of flour in the dough! The bread was edible, but rather crumbly and dry.*

## INGREDIENTS

**5** cups warm water, divided

**1** tablespoon + ⅔ cup sugar, divided

**2** tablespoons active dry yeast

**6** tablespoons oil or shortening, melted

**2** tablespoons salt

**14** cups occident flour

## INSTRUCTIONS

Mix 1 cup warm water, 1 tablespoon sugar, and yeast together and set aside for 10 minutes. In a big bowl, mix oil, salt, remaining 4 cups warm water, and remaining ⅔ cup sugar. Add yeast mixture and stir well. Add flour and stir to make dough. Knead 10 minutes. Allow to rise until double in bowl, covered with tea towel. Shape into 6 loaves and place in greased loaf pans. Allow to rise again until almost double. Bake at 350° for 30 minutes.

## Lucy's Kitchen Tip

Just after removing homemade bread from the oven, cover the loaf in the pan with a tea towel for about 10 minutes. The bread will then slip easily out of the pan.

# Mother's Oatmeal Bread

**Makes 4 loaves**

*Mom and her sister had a birthing center, and Mom made this favorite oatmeal bread to feed the women. The ladies always said, "The bread you made is so good!"*

*Once Mom let it rise too far, and one of the helpers saw it ballooning out over the bowl and onto the floor. She wrapped it in a shawl and threw it out. That was the last of that batch of bread!*

## INGREDIENTS

**3½** cups boiling water

**2** cups quick oats

**1** cup honey

**2** tablespoons salt

**1** cup warm water

**2** tablespoons active dry yeast

**4** eggs

**¾** cup vegetable oil

**4** cups whole wheat flour

**8–10** cups all-purpose flour

## INSTRUCTIONS

Mix boiling water with oats, honey, and salt. Let stand 15 minutes, or until lukewarm. Mix yeast with warm water. Allow to sit a few minutes, and then add to oatmeal mixture with eggs and oil. Beat. Stir in flour to make a soft dough. Knead. Form 4 loaves and put in greased loaf pans. Allow to rise again until almost doubled. Bake 30 minutes at 350°.

# Honey Oatmeal Bread

**Makes 2 loaves**

*At school we pupils and the teacher always repeated this little rhyming prayer before lunchtime:*

*For health and strength and daily bread*
*We praise Thy name, O Lord*
*We thank Thee for this bountiful spread*
*And for Thy precious Word.*

*But at home, we always just bowed our heads in silence to ask the blessing, and then after the meal was over, we bowed our heads again for a silent returning of thanks.*

*I remember once when we had company for supper, I was talking to my cousin and missed the reminder that it was time to pray. I heard a horse and buggy going past the house and turned my head to look out. "It's neighbor Amos driving his new saddle bred," I announced loudly. No one replied, and suddenly I noticed that everything was real quiet. To my embarrassment, they all had their heads bowed for prayer and were trying not to smile.*

## INGREDIENTS

- **3** cups white flour, divided
- **2** tablespoons active dry yeast
- **1½** teaspoon salt
- **1** cup water
- **1** cup cottage cheese
- **4** tablespoons butter
- **½** cup honey
- **2** eggs
- **2½** cups whole wheat flour
- **½** cup rolled oats
- **⅔** cup nuts, chopped

## INSTRUCTIONS

In a large bowl combine 2 cups white flour with yeast and salt. Heat water, cottage cheese, butter, and honey until warm (about 120°). Add warm liquid and eggs to flour mixture. Mix well. Add whole wheat flour, oats, and nuts. Stir in remaining 1 cup white flour. Knead until smooth and elastic. Let rise in greased bowl until double. Punch down. Form into loaves and place in greased loaf pans. Let rise again about 1 hour. Bake at 350° for 35–40 minutes.

# Sesame Onion Braid

## Makes 2 long loaves

*My hobby is browsing through cookbooks and trying new recipes. I must have handed down this trait to my son—he often pages through a cookbook and says, "Mom, make this for supper." He has already given me five cookbooks for Mother's Day, birthdays, and so on.*

*This onion braid is especially good served with a hot soup. Even the family members who don't like onions still enjoy this onion braid.*

*It is also very good to use for sandwiches. Spread slices with onion butter, then bologna, cheese, and lettuce. Our teenage boys who carry lunches really enjoy this for something different. It takes ideas to keep their meals interesting!*

### INGREDIENTS

- **1** tablespoon active dry yeast
- **1¼** cup warm water (110°–115°), divided
- **1** cup sour cream, room temperature
- **3** eggs
- **2** tablespoons (1 envelope) onion soup mix
- **2** tablespoons butter, softened
- **2** tablespoons sugar
- **2** teaspoons salt
- **¼** teaspoon baking soda
- **6½–6¾** cups all-purpose flour
- **1** tablespoon cold water
- **3** tablespoons sesame seeds

### INSTRUCTIONS

In a mixing bowl, dissolve yeast in ¼ cup warm water; let stand for 5 minutes. Add sour cream, 2 eggs, onion soup mix, butter, sugar, salt, baking soda, and remaining 1 cup warm water. Mix well. Stir in enough flour to form a soft dough. Turn onto a floured surface; knead until smooth and elastic, about 6–8 minutes. Place dough in a greased bowl, turning once to grease top. Cover and let rise in a warm place until doubled, about 1 hour. Punch down dough. Turn onto a lightly floured surface and divide into six portions. Shape each into a 15-inch rope. Make 2 braided loaves, pinching ends to seal. Place on greased baking sheets. Cover and let rise until doubled, about 1 hour. Beat cold water and the remaining egg. Brush over dough. Sprinkle with sesame seeds. Bake at 350° for 35–40 minutes, or until golden brown.

# English Muffin Loaves

**Makes 2 loaves**

*Over the years, time and again, we've been glad for this recipe. It's easier and takes less time than our usual bread recipe. So sometimes when we need bread quickly, we go for this. It's also good for gifts, or for a token of appreciation when someone does you a favor, such as the man who brought our dog back.*

*For seven years now we've had two dogs, Holly and Heidi. One evening a truck driver brought us a piece of machinery. Holly apparently got on the trailer without anyone noticing. Later we realized she was missing and didn't know what happened. A week later Dad met the driver again and asked him about Holly. Sure enough, the driver told us she raced off his trailer when he opened it about one hundred miles from home. He said he'd bring her back to us if anyone found her. We also put an ad in Die Botschaft.*

*Later we received a letter informing us that some people were keeping Holly for us. She came to them when it was thundering—she has always been afraid of thunder. About six weeks after she left, the same driver brought her back. We sure rejoiced to have our dog back!*

## INGREDIENTS

**5½–6** cups flour, divided

**2** tablespoons active dry yeast

**1** tablespoon sugar

**2** teaspoons salt

**¼** teaspoon baking soda

**2** cups milk

**½** cup water

cornmeal

## INSTRUCTIONS

Combine 3 cups flour, yeast, sugar, salt, and baking soda. Heat liquids until very warm (120°–130°). Add to dry mixture and beat well. Stir in up to 3 cups flour to make a stiff batter. Spoon into 8½ x 4½-inch loaf pans that have been greased and sprinkled with cornmeal. Sprinkle tops with cornmeal. Cover. Let rise in warm place for 45 minutes. Bake at 400° for 25 minutes. Remove from pans immediately and cool.

## Note

Be sure to measure flour by spooning lightly into the cup; otherwise you get too much in the recipe and the bread gets dry.

# Hot Cross Buns

**Makes 24 buns**

## INGREDIENTS

- **1** cup warm milk
- **1** cup warm water
- **1** tablespoon active dry yeast
- **½** cup sugar
- **2** eggs
- **½** cup butter or margarine, softened
- **1** teaspoon salt
- **7–8** cups flour, enough for a stiff dough

## INSTRUCTIONS

Mix milk, water, and yeast together. Stir in sugar, eggs, butter, and salt. Add flour a cup at a time until dough comes together. Knead 10 minutes. Divide into 24 rolls and arrange in two greased 9 x 13-inch cake pans. With a sharp knife, slash an *X* on top of each roll. Let rise until double and bake 25 minutes at 350°. Frost with your favorite frosting and enjoy!

# Pecan Rolls

## Makes about 18 rolls

*My cousin made these pecan rolls for a skating party at my uncle's place last winter, and everyone liked them—especially my brothers, who ate the most! So I got the recipe from my cousin, who is my age. Of course all of us were probably extra-hungry from all that exercise in the frosty, cold air, which made them taste better.*

*We played crack-the-whip and prisoner's base that night under the full moon. The ice was super-smooth and didn't have a bit of snow on it. A boy asked my eighteen-year-old cousin for a date, so the evening was extra-special for her, too. They were skating together for a while, and we teased and whistled at them. These pecan rolls, along with mugs of hot chocolate, sure tasted good when we got back to the warm kitchen.*

### INGREDIENTS

**3¾** cups flour, divided
**2** tablespoons active dry yeast
**¾** cup milk
**½** cup water
**¼** cup margarine
**¼** cup sugar
**1** egg
**½** teaspoon salt

*Topping:*
**¾** cup margarine
**1** cup brown sugar
**1** tablespoon Karo syrup
**1** teaspoon cinnamon
**1** tablespoon water
**½** cup pecans, chopped

### INSTRUCTIONS

Place 1½ cup flour in bowl. Add yeast and stir. In saucepan, measure milk, water, margarine, sugar, and egg. Stir just until margarine is melted. Allow to cool to lukewarm. Pour over yeast and flour and stir. Add rest of flour and salt to make a soft dough. Knead briefly. Let rise in greased bowl until double. Pinch off balls of dough and form into rolls. Make topping: Melt margarine. Add brown sugar, Karo syrup, cinnamon, water, and pecans. Spread in a 9 x 13-inch pan. Lay rolls on top and let rise again until nearly double. Bake at 350° for 22–25 minutes. Flip hot pan onto tray or platter so that gooey pecan mixture is now on top of the rolls, running down their sides.

# Oatmeal Nut Sticky Buns

**Makes 24 buns**

*This is my favorite sticky bun recipe. They sure are delicious, especially when still warm. I like to bake pans to give to the neighbors at Christmas. We have close neighbors on all four sides of us in our small town.*

*One year for a Christmas cookie exchange, for something different, I baked each a pan of these instead of a plateful of cookies.*

## INGREDIENTS

- ⅓ cup warm water
- 1 tablespoon active dry yeast
- 1 cup milk
- ⅓ cup shortening
- 1¾ cup sugar, divided
- 1 teaspoon salt
- 2 eggs, beaten
- 1 cup quick oats
- 4–4½ cups occident or bread flour, divided
- 6 tablespoons melted butter, plus a little more to brush on the dough
- 2 tablespoons mild molasses or maple syrup
- 1 cup nuts, chopped
- ½ cup brown sugar
- 2 teaspoons cinnamon

## Note

May replace nuts with raisins. May use part whole wheat flour.

## INSTRUCTIONS

Combine water and yeast. Stir and set aside. Scald milk and put in the shortening to melt; stir. Cool to lukewarm and pour into large bowl. Add ½ cup sugar, salt, and eggs. Add yeast mixture. Add oats and 1 cup flour. Beat well with mixer or by hand. Add more flour to make a soft dough, and knead until smooth and elastic. Place in greased bowl and butter top of dough. Cover and let rise until double in bulk. Punch down, cover, and let rest 10 minutes.

Prepare pans. Place 6 tablespoons melted butter, molasses, ¾ cup sugar, and nuts evenly in 3 round cake pans (8- or 9-inch). Then divide dough in half and roll out each half into a 12-inch square. Brush with melted butter. Mix together remaining ½ cup sugar, brown sugar, and cinnamon. Sprinkle evenly on both squares of dough. Roll each square into a log. Cut into 12 (1-inch) pieces.

Place 8 rolls on top of the syrup and nuts in each pan. Cover and let rise until double again. Bake at 350° for 18–20 minutes, until lightly browned. Invert on plates a few minutes after removing from oven so sticky topping runs down over the buns where it belongs and doesn't stick in the pans.

# Cinnamon Fruit Buns

**Makes 3 (9 x 13-inch) pans of buns**

*This recipe was given to me by a dear niece who is seventeen years younger than I am but seems more like a sister. We often share recipes and ideas about cooking and baking. One day she came to our house with these delicious fruit buns. From then on, our children clap and cheer when they come into the kitchen and I am rolling out these fruit buns!*

*We've tried them with different fruit toppings—cherry, strawberry, apple, and pineapple—and they're all delicious. I've made the buns for many different occasions—frolics, quiltings, Sisters' Day, and school get-togethers. I've also given them as Christmas gifts to the neighbors, or when there's a new baby in a home, and also for young folks' gathering. Often, the result is: "May I have your recipe?"*

## INGREDIENTS

- **2** cups mashed potatoes
- **1** cup shortening or oil
- **1** cup sugar
- **2** tablespoons salt
- **1** quart milk, scalded
- **½** cup warm water
- **3** tablespoons active dry yeast
- **2** eggs
- **7½** cups bread flour
- **7½** cups all-purpose flour
- butter, softened
- brown sugar
- cinnamon
- **3** (20-ounce) cans fruit filling

*Glaze*

- **1** cup butter, melted
- **6** cups confectioners' sugar
- **4** teaspoons vanilla
- **6–8** tablespoons hot water

## INSTRUCTIONS

Mix mashed potatoes, shortening, sugar, salt, and scalded milk. Cool to lukewarm. Dissolve yeast in warm water. Add to milk mixture with eggs and flour. Mix well and knead. Let rise until double in bulk. Roll out dough. Spread with softened butter and sprinkle brown sugar and cinnamon on dough. Roll up, slice ¾ inch thick, and place in 3 greased 9 x 13-inch cake pans. Let rise about 30 minutes. Spread with fruit filling, 1 can per pan. Bake 25–30 minutes at 350°. Cool. Mix glaze ingredients. Glaze cooled buns.

## Lucy's Kitchen Tip

If not everyone at your table likes cinnamon, keep some mixed with a bit of sugar in a salt shaker to sprinkle on applesauce, apple tarts, rhubarb jam, and the like.

# Mama's Cinnamon Buns

**Makes 2 (11 x 15-inch) pans**

*Mama's Cinnamon Buns used to be one of my favorite comfort foods when I was a schoolgirl. When I came home from school and caught a whiff of the tantalizing aroma of freshly baked warm buns and cinnamon icing glaze, I would start to ransack the cupboards in search of them. My older sister, who was so good at making these buns—and even better at hiding them—didn't want me to sample any until we were at the supper table. I remember how delighted I was once when I found them hidden on the top shelf in the fruit cellar!*

## INGREDIENTS

- **3** tablespoons active dry yeast
- **½** cup warm water
- **1** cup margarine
- **3** cups milk, scalded
- **5** eggs
- **1** cup sugar
- **2** teaspoons salt
- **11–12** cups flour
   butter, softened
   cinnamon
   brown sugar

*Frosting*

- **1** cup margarine
- **2** cups brown sugar
- **⅔** cup milk
   confectioners' sugar
- **1** teaspoon cinnamon

## INSTRUCTIONS

Dissolve yeast in warm water. Put margarine in milk after it is scalded. Set aside until lukewarm. Beat eggs and sugar. Add salt, yeast, and milk. Add the flour. The dough will be quite sticky. Let rise until double in size. Divide dough in half and roll out into rectangle. Spread with softened butter and sprinkle with cinnamon and brown sugar. Roll up and cut into 1-inch pieces. Place in two 11 x 15-inch greased pans and allow to rise again. Bake at 350° for 20–25 minutes. Make frosting: Melt margarine. Add brown sugar and milk. Heat just enough so sugar dissolves. Set aside until cool. Add confectioners' sugar and cinnamon. Do not stir while cooling. Frost buns.

# Delicious Rolls with Penuche Icing

**Makes about 36 rolls**

*Before I got married ten years ago, I gave each of my friends a recipe card to fill out and give back to me. Thus I had a nice variety of recipes when I got married. Now this roll recipe is one of my favorites and often brings compliments because they are so delicious.*

*My friend who gave me this recipe died from leukemia at the young age of thirty-five. I like to remember her every time I make these rolls. On the recipe card, she also wrote this verse:*

*It's the little things we do and say*
*That mean so much as we go our way.*
*A kindly deed can lift a load*
*From weary shoulders on the road.*

*And that is exactly as I remember her. She was always kind and friendly.*

## INGREDIENTS

*Rolls*

**1**   cup hot water

**½**   cup sugar

**1½** teaspoon salt

**½**   cup margarine

**2**   tablespoons active dry yeast

**1**   cup lukewarm water

**2**   eggs, well beaten

**6–7** cups flour

      butter

      cinnamon

. . . . . . . .

*Penuche Icing*

**½**   cup butter

**½**   cup white sugar

**½**   cup brown sugar, packed

**¼**   cup milk

**1¾–2** cups confectioners' sugar, sifted

## INSTRUCTIONS

Pour hot water over sugar, salt, and margarine. Dissolve yeast in lukewarm water. Add yeast and eggs. Beat well. Gradually add flour just until a soft dough forms. Knead into soft, elastic dough, softer dough than for bread. Let rise in greased bowl, covered, in a warm place until double in size. Knead briefly and let rise again. Roll out and spread generously with butter. Sprinkle cinnamon to your liking. Roll up as for jelly roll and cut into slices. Place in greased pans. Let rise for about 1 hour. Bake at 350° for 15–20 minutes, just so they start to brown slightly. Ice when cool.

. . . . . . .

Melt butter in saucepan. Add white and brown sugars. Boil and stir over low heat for 2 minutes. Add milk. Bring back to a boil, stirring constantly. Cool to lukewarm. Gradually add confectioners' sugar. Add a splash of vanilla, if desired. Place hot pan in ice water and stir until thick enough to spread.

# No-Knead Refrigerator Rolls

**Makes about 3 dozen rolls**

*I get nice, soft rolls when this dough sits in the refrigerator overnight or several days. One New Year's Day, I had invited friends for dinner. I mixed these rolls the evening before, intending to bake them shortly before the guests came. I guess I didn't allow them enough time to warm up, because they didn't rise well and were tough. Guests were here and the meal was ready, so I served them without apologies, but it was one of my most embarrassing moments. My guests glanced at me as they ate them, but no one said anything about them in my presence. After that I knew the rolls needed to rise until double in bulk, just like other yeast recipes.*

## INGREDIENTS

**2** cups boiling water

**½** cup sugar

**1** tablespoon salt

**2** tablespoons shortening

**2** eggs, beaten

**2** tablespoons active dry yeast

**¼** cup warm water

**8** cups flour, divided

## INSTRUCTIONS

Stir together boiling water, sugar, salt, and shortening. Let cool to lukewarm. Add eggs. Separately, mix together yeast and water. Add to first mixture. Add 4 cups flour and beat well. Add rest of flour and mix well. Form into balls and place on baking sheets to let rise until double. Bake at 400° until golden brown, about 15 minutes. This dough can be stored in refrigerator until needed; just form into balls and let rise. Delicious!

# Egg Rusks

**Makes about 4 dozen rolls**

*These were a childhood favorite of mine, very delicious with butter and molasses spread over them. Food was a magnet to me as a child. Whenever I walked past food, I always had an urge to sample some. Once when Mom saw me eating she exclaimed, "You'll get to be as fat as Grandma!" I guess I already knew girls want to be slim, as I desperately hoped I wouldn't get fat like Grandma. Thus I started to think before eating food at my fingertips and before stuffing myself at the table. Later I learned that some foods are less fattening than others, and healthier, too.*

### INGREDIENTS

- **1** tablespoon active dry yeast
- **1** cup warm water
- **1** cup mashed potatoes
- **4** eggs
- **1** cup sugar
- **5–7** cups bread flour, divided

### INSTRUCTIONS

Mix yeast, water, potatoes, eggs, sugar, and 2 cups flour in evening. Cover and let rise. Next morning, stir down. Add about 3 more cups flour to make dough just dry enough to handle and knead. Form into buns and place in greased pan to rise until double. Bake at 350° for 30 minutes, or until done.

# Soft Dinner Rolls

## Makes 32 rolls

*These rolls always seem to turn out right—soft and good. That is, if I don't forget to bake them. Once, I had the dough rising in a bowl on the counter and was intending to soon punch it down to shape into rolls. About that time there was a knock at the door, and there stood our son-in-law, who lived just a quarter mile down the road. He announced the surprise arrival of a baby son to him and our daughter, two weeks early. Their first baby! We had planned for me to go help them out the first few days, and I was eager to go. In my excitement and rush to get ready, I forgot all about my rolls. That evening when my hubby came home, the dough had risen out over the bowl and fallen to the floor!*

### INGREDIENTS

- **1** cup milk
- **½** cup butter
- **2** eggs, beaten
- **¾** cup sugar
- **1** cup warm water
- **2** tablespoons active dry yeast
- **2** teaspoons salt
- **6–7** cups bread flour

### INSTRUCTIONS

Scald the milk and add the butter to melt. Cool to luke-warm. Add eggs, sugar, warm water, yeast, and salt. Mix. Add flour until dough forms. Knead 10 minutes. Let rise 1 hour in greased bowl, covered. Divide dough in half, and keep dividing each portion in half until there are 32 pieces. Shape into rolls and put on greased baking sheets. Cover. Let rise until double in bulk. Bake at 400° for 15–20 minutes.

# Breadsticks

**Serves 4–6**

One of my favorite hobbies is collecting recipes and trying out new ones. I really enjoy baking and cooking for our family of ten—six boys and four girls.

I usually serve our family a special Christmas supper eaten by candlelight, and I enjoy trying a new dish or something different to surprise them. One year I made cheese sticks, but they turned out a bit on the dry side and were a big disappointment for this mother, who thought she was making something fancy!

After hearing folks talk about delicious Pizza Hut breadsticks, I decided to try my hand at making my own recipe. So I searched my cookbooks and combined three recipes into one. And the result was cheers from everyone!

## INGREDIENTS

- **1½** cup warm water
- **1** tablespoon active dry yeast
- **1** tablespoon oil
- **1** tablespoon sugar
- **1¼** teaspoon salt
- **4** cups bread flour
- **3** cups mozzarella cheese, grated
- **2** tablespoons dried parsley
- **2** tablespoons dried oregano
- **1** teaspoon garlic powder
- **1** cup butter, melted
  pizza sauce, for serving

## INSTRUCTIONS

Mix yeast and warm water and let stand for a few minutes. Add rest of ingredients except the butter and pizza sauce. Mix. Let rise until double (if I'm in a hurry, I use it before it rises that much). Roll out ¼–½ inch thick. Cut into 1-inch strips. Twist 2 or 3 times. Rolls twists in melted butter. Then put on greased pan, 2 inches apart. Bake at 400° for 15–20 minutes, until crusty brown. Serve with warm pizza sauce for dipping.

# Favorite Soft Pretzels

**Serves 6**

*This is a favorite recipe for our family of six children. Soft pretzels are often our Sunday evening supper or snack. Served with cheese and chocolate milk, they're a real treat anytime!*

## INGREDIENTS

**1** tablespoon active dry yeast

**¾** cup warm water

**¼** teaspoon salt

**1** tablespoon brown sugar

**2½** cups flour

**1** teaspoon baking soda

**1** cup water

coarse salt

butter, melted

## INSTRUCTIONS

Dissolve yeast in warm water and let stand 5 minutes. Add salt, brown sugar, and flour. Mix and knead until a soft dough is formed. Shape into pretzels. Combine baking soda and water. Dip each pretzel in baking soda solution. Place on a greased baking sheet and sprinkle with coarse salt. Bake at 475° for 10–12 minutes. Brush with melted butter.

## Note

Sometimes I use part whole wheat flour. Also, I sometimes sprinkle sour cream and onion or cheddar cheese powder on them after they are dipped in butter.

# Elizabeth's Soft Pretzels

**Serves 6**

*This recipe tastes more like Auntie Anne's soft pretzels than any other I've ever tasted. Our daughters have often made these for get-togethers—and they sure do bring smiles! Telling our neighbors we're making soft pretzels is a good way to make them show up on our doorstep.*

## INGREDIENTS

- **1** cup warm water
- **1** tablespoon active dry yeast
- **1** tablespoon brown sugar
- **2** cups all-purpose flour
- **1** cup occident flour
- **4** tablespoons baking soda, dissolved in **4** cups water
- coarse salt
- butter

## INSTRUCTIONS

Combine warm water, yeast, brown sugar, and flour. Knead into dough. Shape into pretzels. Dip pretzels into baking soda water. Then put on baking sheets. Sprinkle with salt. Bake at 450° for 12–15 minutes. Brush with butter several times while baking.

# Crème-Filled Doughnuts

**Makes 30 doughnuts**

## INGREDIENTS

**2** cups lukewarm water

**1** tablespoon active dry yeast

**½** cup vegetable oil

**½** cup sugar

**2** eggs, well beaten

**2** teaspoons salt

**6** cups flour (approximately)

. . . . . . .

*E-Z Frosting for Filling*

**½** cup shortening

**½** cup butter

**¾** cup sugar

**7** tablespoons flour

**1** teaspoon vanilla

**½** cup milk

## INSTRUCTIONS

Mix water, yeast, oil, sugar, eggs, and salt in big bowl. Add just enough flour so that dough is still a little sticky but smooth. Knead. Let rise in greased bowl until double. Pat the dough out, and then use the rolling pin lightly and sparingly. Let rise again. Cut out doughnuts. Fry in hot fat or oil at 375°, deep enough so doughnuts float. (Don't have your oil too hot, or doughnuts will have doughy centers.) Remove hot doughnuts to paper towel–lined plates. Use a paring knife to poke a hole in the side. Fill with E-Z Frosting in a pastry bag with a long tip.

. . . . . . .

Put all ingredients in a bowl and let stand 30 minutes. Then beat 5 minutes.

## Note

This dough recipe can also be used for sticky buns, which is what I do with my scraps.

# Delicious Doughnuts

**Makes about 3 dozen doughnuts**

*Doughnuts always bring back a bittersweet memory of when pride went before a fall. I believe I was nineteen, and my sister was one and a half years younger. I felt myself the wiser and more superior one.*

*We decided to have the youth for a singing, and, because we lived in Lancaster County, that could be quite a number of people. I decided on doughnuts as a treat, and I also declared that to be sure they were good enough, I'd make them all myself.*

*Mom decided differently—my sister and I would each make half. I relented rather reluctantly, because our reputation was at stake! What if my sister goofed it up? However, I forgot to put the salt in my dough, and my doughnuts tasted flat and hers were good. And because so many people came for the singing, we had to serve my goofed-up doughnuts, too.*

*Every time I make doughnuts, I remember when the older, wiser, more superior sister got humbled!*

## INGREDIENTS

- **2** tablespoons active dry yeast
- **½** cup + **1** tablespoon sugar, divided
- **2¼** cups warm water, divided
- **1** cup shortening
- **2** eggs
- **2** teaspoons salt
- **1** cup warm potato water (heat to boiling first and allow to cool)
- **7–8** cups flour

## INSTRUCTIONS

Dissolve yeast and 1 tablespoon sugar in ¼ cup warm water. Let stand 10 minutes. In a large bowl, combine shortening, eggs, remaining ½ cup sugar, and salt. Add remaining 2 cups water and potato water. (If potato water isn't available, just use a total of 3 cups water). Mix well, then add yeast mixture and mix.

Add flour, stirring after every 2 cups until dough is soft but not sticky. Let rise in a warm place until double in size, about 1 hour. Knead well. Roll out gently, and cut into doughnuts. Cover and let rise about 1 hour. Fry in hot oil (about 375°) and drain on paper towels. Dip in sugar while warm.

# Potato Doughnuts

**Makes about 4 dozen doughnuts**

*Every year in April, our church people go together and have a big yard and bake sale to help with hospital expenses. My mother usually has some of her cream-filled doughnuts there. There are never any left over—people just snatch them up.*

*And every year, my dad has a three-day sale in his shop. We make free coffee and doughnuts for the customers, usually about six hundred doughnuts for those three days. The people often have some kind of a compliment about the good doughnuts.*

### INGREDIENTS

**2** tablespoons active dry yeast

½ cup warm water

**2** cups scalded milk, cooled to room temperature

½ cup shortening

½ cup sugar

**2** teaspoons salt

**1½–2** cups mashed potatoes

**4** eggs, beaten

**10–12** cups flour

. . . . . . .

*Doughnut Filling*

**2** egg whites

**4** cups confectioners' sugar

**2** teaspoons vanilla

**4** tablespoons flour

**4** tablespoons milk

**1½** cup shortening

### INSTRUCTIONS

Mix together, using the lesser amount of flour for a soft yet workable dough. Knead until smooth and satiny. Place in lightly greased bowl, turning to grease top. Cover. Let rise until doubled. Roll into large square and cut with cutter or floured scissors. Allow to rise briefly. Don't let them rise too long until you start frying them, as they do rise while frying. Fry them in hot oil (about 375°) with the top turned down. Remove to paper towel–lined trays. Fill doughnuts with filling and roll in doughnut sugar.

. . . . . . .

Beat egg whites into soft peaks. Add sugar and vanilla. Add rest of ingredients and beat well.

# Overnight Doughnuts

## Makes about 8 dozen doughnuts

*This is a very old recipe of mine. When our six children were little, on the day of our neighbors' annual yard sale, I'd get up at four o'clock in the morning to cut and fry them, and I'd be done by seven o'clock in the morning, in time for the sale. Every year people would come just for these doughnuts. One man bought six and ate them right away!*

### INGREDIENTS

**1** cup mashed potatoes

**4** tablespoons sugar

**2** teaspoons salt

**4** cups potato water (bring to a boil first, then cool down)

**2** tablespoons active dry yeast

**½** cup warm water

. . . . . . .

**8** eggs, room temperature

**4** cups warm potato water

**3** cups sugar

**3** cups oil

**20** cups flour (approximately)

### INSTRUCTIONS

Mix together at 5 p.m. Cover. Let rise until bedtime. Then add ingredients below.

. . . . . . .

Knead until elastic. Allow to stand overnight, covered. In the morning, knead and roll out. Cut into doughnuts. Let rise, and fry in oil (375°). Drain on paper towels. Dip in sugar or glaze.

# Sisters' Day Doughnuts and Glaze

**Makes about 4 dozen doughnuts**

*Doughnut Day! It's a day to look forward to during the long winter days and weeks. On Mom's birthday in December every year, my sisters bring their supplies to our basement, to the sink down there.*

*We like having our carry-in lunch upstairs in the kitchen, so we can stay out of the doughnuts' way. It's usually a crowd with six mothers, me, and Mom. At least twelve children and babies are running around putting fingerprints in the rising doughnuts. Some of the doughnuts at the outer edge of the table have funny shapes sometimes!*

*Each sister and sister-in-law makes at least two hundred to three hundred doughnuts, some filled and some glazed. We like to mix pie filling with icing for the filled ones.*

*Of course a lot of doughnuts get eaten while at their best—fresh and warm. At the end of the day, no one wants to see or eat another doughnut for a day or two. But each heads home with sleepy children and lots of yummy doughnuts—and precious memories, of course. Work goes faster when you can talk with your sisters.*

## INGREDIENTS

- **1** cup warm water
- **4** tablespoons active dry yeast
- **4** cups warm milk
- **1** cup sugar
- **1** cup shortening
- **4** eggs
- **1** tablespoon salt
- **12** cups bread flour

. . . . . . .

*Glaze for Doughnuts*

- **1** pound confectioners' sugar
- **2** tablespoons cornstarch
- **2** tablespoons butter
- **2** tablespoons vanilla
- **4** tablespoons milk

## INSTRUCTIONS

Combine water and yeast. Let stand 15 minutes. Add remaining ingredients. For extra softness, you may add a pack of instant mashed potatoes (prepared as on box)—before adding all the flour. Dough will be a little sticky and does not need much kneading. Use plenty of flour to roll out. Cut doughnuts. Allow to rise briefly. Fry in hot oil (375°) and drain on paper towels. Glaze with following recipe.

. . . . . . .

Mix. Add milk by tablespoon until the desired consistency.

# Betsey's Blueberry Muffins

**Makes 16–20 muffins**

I got this muffin recipe from my cousins who had joined us for a picnic in the woods one Sunday and brought some of these muffins along. There was an old picnic table in the clearing, on which we put all our grub while we explored. It was such a lovely, breezy day and too early for lunch, so we followed the noisy little brook, wading through ferns and mayapples. Soon we heard a splashing sound of falling water and came upon a miniature waterfall! We were so enchanted by it that we almost forgot about eating lunch.

When we got back to the picnic table, there were two chipmunks on it, stirring around in our things. They scampered off and darted away in the woods. We decided that next time we'd bring some corn or seeds for them.

## INGREDIENTS

- **3** cups flour
- **4** teaspoons baking powder
- **1** teaspoon salt
- **1** cup sugar
- **¼** cup brown sugar
- **2** eggs
- **1** cup milk
- **½** cup vegetable oil
- **2** cups blueberries
- **¼** cup pecans, chopped

## INSTRUCTIONS

Sift flour. Add baking powder, salt, and sugars. Separately, beat eggs, milk, and oil together. Stir wet ingredients into dry only enough to blend together; batter should appear slightly lumpy. Fold in blueberries and pecans. Spoon into greased muffin tins. Bake at 375° for 25 minutes.

# Apple Raisin Muffins

**Makes 16 muffins**

### INGREDIENTS

½   cup whole wheat flour

1½ cup flour

1¼ cup sugar

2   teaspoons baking soda

½   teaspoon salt

2   cups carrots, grated

½   cup raisins

½   cup nuts, chopped

½   cup grated coconut

1   apple, peeled and grated

3   eggs

1   cup vegetable oil

2   teaspoons vanilla

### INSTRUCTIONS

In a large bowl mix flours, sugar, baking soda, and salt. Stir in carrots, raisins, nuts, coconut, and apple. Separately, mix eggs, oil, and vanilla together. Stir egg mixture into flour mixture until batter is just combined. Spoon into well-greased muffin tins, filling to the top. Bake at 350° for 20 minutes.

# Drop Biscuits

**Makes 15 small biscuits**

### INGREDIENTS

2   cups flour

4   teaspoons baking powder

½   teaspoon salt

4   tablespoons butter or shortening

1   cup milk

### INSTRUCTIONS

Put dry ingredients together. Add shortening and mix with fork. Add milk to make a soft dough. Drop by spoonful into a buttered cake pan. Bake at 475° for 11–14 minutes.

# Whole Wheat Muffins

**Makes 16 muffins**

## INGREDIENTS

**2** cups whole wheat pastry flour

¼ cup wheat germ

¾ cup quick oats

¼ cup raisins

**1** teaspoon baking powder

**1** teaspoon baking soda

**1½** teaspoon cinnamon

⅓ cup molasses

⅔ cup honey

⅓ cup vegetable oil

**1** egg

**1** cup water

## INSTRUCTIONS

Combine dry ingredients. Separately combine liquid ingredients. Stir wet mixture into dry mixture, mixing very little. Do not beat. Spoon batter into paper-lined or greased muffin cups. Bake at 350° for 15 minutes, or until springy when touched lightly.

# Katie's Corn Bread

**Serves 4–6**

## INGREDIENTS

**2** eggs

**2** tablespoons vegetable oil

**1** cup milk

¾ cup yellow cornmeal

**1** cup all-purpose flour

**3½** teaspoons baking powder

**2** tablespoons sugar

**1** teaspoon salt

## INSTRUCTIONS

Beat eggs. Add oil and milk. Stir in dry ingredients. Mix well. Pour into greased 8 x 10-inch pan. Bake at 375° for 25–30 minutes.

Soups,
sandwiches,
& Pizza

## Clayton's Beef Stew

**Serves 4**

### INGREDIENTS

- **1** quart canned beef chunks with broth
- **4** medium carrots, diced
- **1** medium onion, diced
- **5** medium potatoes, diced
- **1** small bell pepper, diced
- **2** cups water
- **4** tablespoons flour
- **½** cup vegetable oil
- salt and pepper, to taste

### INSTRUCTIONS

Cook beef, carrots, onions, potatoes, bell pepper, and water together in Dutch oven on low heat until the vegetables are tender, 30–60 minutes. Separately, brown flour to deep brown in vegetable oil. Add brown flour thickening to stew, and salt and pepper, to taste. Cook over medium heat, stirring frequently, until thickened.

### Note

We like it with some seasonings—like hot pepper (sparingly) or seasoned salt.

## Beef Barley Soup

**Serves 6–8**

### INGREDIENTS

- **2** quarts beef and broth
- **1** quart tomatoes
- **1½** cup barley
- **1** cup carrots, chopped
- **1** cup potatoes, diced
- **1** cup celery, chopped
- **½** cup onion, chopped
- **¼** cup parsley, chopped
- **½** teaspoon thyme
- **1** teaspoon basil
- salt and pepper, to taste

### INSTRUCTIONS

Cook together in kettle for 1 hour or so until barley is soft. Stir once in a while as barley thickens. Can be cooked in slow cooker on low for 5–6 hours.

# Garden Vegetable Soup

**Serves 4–6**

*This vegetable soup recipe is our favorite. We usually have it Saturday for the noon meal. It's best in the summertime when we have fresh garden vegetables to put in—new sugar peas, little carrots, and fresh cabbage. Or later in the summer—fresh limas, corn, and tomatoes, which make it especially delicious. When fresh tomatoes aren't in season we use canned tomato juice.*

*Last summer when I was at the birth center with our eleventh baby, our oldest daughter, age thirteen, made this soup because she thought it would be easier than making a full-course meal. As she found out, gathering the vegetables from the garden and preparing them took longer than she had planned. When Dad and the hired man came in for dinner, the vegetables weren't soft yet. They had to go back outside and work for another half hour. But when they tasted the soup, they said it was well worth the wait!*

## INGREDIENTS

**2–3** pounds meaty soup bones
**1** tablespoon salt
pepper, to taste
**2** bouillon cubes
**2** quarts water
**1** cup cabbage, shredded
**2** potatoes, peeled and diced
**¼** teaspoon thyme or marjoram
**2** ribs celery, sliced
**2** carrots, sliced
**1** small onion, chopped
**2** cups fresh or canned tomatoes

## INSTRUCTIONS

Cover and simmer soup bones, salt, pepper, bouillon, and water for 2½–3 hours. Remove bones. Return meat to soup and add vegetables. Simmer approximately 30 minutes more.

# California Chowder

**Serves 6–8**

*Several years ago we had a small donkey given to us by an English [non-Amish] friend. He was cute, but he had a habit of braying at any time of the day or night. We hadn't realized how irksome this was to the neighbors a quarter mile down the road until one morning when we saw a paper taped against the outside barn door: "If you don't strangle that donkey, I will!"*

*That decided it. The donkey was sent to the sale barn the very next Monday. A few days later the neighbor lady came and brought us a pot of soup. She probably felt guilty about her husband having put that on the barn door and wanted to make amends. I later got the soup recipe from her, and we're still very good friends.*

## INGREDIENTS

- **3** quarts water
- **1** quart potatoes, cubed
- **1** medium onion, chopped
- **3** ribs celery, sliced
- **3** medium carrots, chopped
- **1** cup cooked beef chunks
- **2** cups beef broth
- **2** teaspoons salt
- **¼** teaspoon oregano
- **¼** teaspoon celery salt
- **¼** teaspoon paprika
- **¼** teaspoon black pepper
- pinch sage
- pinch seasoned salt
- pinch red pepper
- parsley, if desired
- **2** tablespoons flour
- **2** tablespoons water
- **2** tablespoons cream

## INSTRUCTIONS

Combine water, vegetables, beef, and broth in kettle. Bring to boil and simmer for 1–2 hours. Add seasonings. Thicken by whisking together flour, water, and cream and then whisking into soup until thickened.

## Lucy's Kitchen Tip

Chop celery and parsley leaves and freeze them on trays. Place frozen leaves in a freezer container. Just grab a few pinches to add to soups, sauces, and one-dish meals.

# Montana Chowder

**Serves 12**

## INGREDIENTS

- **2** pounds ground beef
- **2** teaspoons salt
- garlic salt, optional
- ⅛ teaspoon pepper
- **2** eggs, beaten
- ¼ cup parsley, chopped
- ½ cup fine cracker or bread crumbs
- **2** tablespoons milk
- **3–5** tablespoons flour
- **1** tablespoon vegetable oil
- **2** bay leaves, optional
- **4–6** small onions, chopped
- **2–3** cups celery, diced
- **3–4** cups potatoes, diced
- ¼ cup long-grain rice
- **6** cups tomato juice
- **6** cups water
- **1** tablespoon sugar
- **1** teaspoon salt
- **1½** cup canned corn

## INSTRUCTIONS

Mix thoroughly meat, salt, garlic salt, pepper, eggs, parsley, crumbs, and milk. Form balls the size of a walnut. Dip in flour. Heat oil in large kettle. Lightly brown meatballs on all sides. Add remaining ingredients except corn. Bring to a boil. Cover and cook slowly until vegetables are tender. Add corn last. Cook 10 minutes.

## Note

Carrots, peas, and celery leaves can be used.

# Chunky Beef Soup

**Serves 6–8**

## INGREDIENTS

- **2½** quarts water
- **⅓** cup beef base
- **1** (15-ounce) can beef broth, optional
- **1** quart tomato juice
- **½** cup sugar
- **1** teaspoon salt
- **1** small onion, chopped
- **½** cup margarine
- **2½** pounds ground beef
- **1** quart carrots, diced
- **1** quart potatoes, diced
- **3** cups frozen or fresh peas
- **2** cups cooked navy beans
  salt and pepper, to taste

## INSTRUCTIONS

Bring water, beef base, broth, tomato juice, sugar, and salt to boil in kettle. Brown onion in margarine. Brown ground beef. Add to kettle with rest of ingredients. Simmer until vegetables are soft.

# Easy Hamburger Soup

**Serves 6**

### INGREDIENTS

- **2** tablespoons butter
- **1** pound ground beef
- **1** cup onion, chopped
- **2** cups tomato juice
- **1** cup carrots, sliced
- **½** cup celery or bell peppers, chopped
- **1** cup potatoes, diced
- **1** teaspoon seasoned salt
- **1–1½** teaspoon salt
- **⅛** teaspoon pepper
- **⅓** cup flour
- **4** cups milk, divided

### INSTRUCTIONS

Melt butter in large skillet or kettle and brown meat and onion. Stir in tomato juice, carrots, celery, potatoes, both salts, and pepper. Cover and simmer until vegetables are tender, approximately 20–25 minutes. Separately, combine flour with 1 cup milk. Stir into soup and boil. Add remaining milk and heat, stirring frequently. Heat until hot, but don't allow to boil.

# Chili Soup

**Serves 8**

### INGREDIENTS

- **1** quart ground beef, canned or fresh
- **1–2** medium onions
- **2** (15-ounce) cans chili beans
- **2** (15-ounce) cans kidney beans
- **2** (10¾-ounce) cans cream of mushroom soup
- **1** (4-ounce) can mushrooms
- **2** bell peppers, chopped
- **2** quarts tomatoes, peeled and chopped
- salt, to taste
- chili powder, to taste

### INSTRUCTIONS

Fry beef and onions together. Add rest of ingredients. Simmer for 1 hour.

# Grandmother's Spaghetti Soup

**Makes about 20 quarts**

*My sister and her husband have seven children under age ten, including a set of twins—and she also has a fabric store to care for. My brother and his wife have seven children too. When we drive down from Pennsylvania to visit them, we fill up a van and go make precious memories. It naturally takes a lot of grub for the gang. So Mom makes batches of spaghetti soup and cans it in two-quart jars. When we're visiting and suddenly it's mealtime, and you have to feed so many people in such short order—spaghetti soup! It's a delicious, quick meal.*

## INGREDIENTS

- **3** pounds dried Great Northern beans
- **3** pounds uncooked spaghetti
- **½** cup butter
- **4** onions, chopped
- **3** ribs celery, diced
- **4** pounds ground beef
- **10–12** quarts tomato juice
- **1** quart carrots, shredded
  salt and brown sugar, to taste

## INSTRUCTIONS

Soak beans overnight, then cook until soft. Drain. Cook spaghetti. Fry onions, celery, and ground beef in melted butter. Mix all together with tomato juice, carrots, salt, and brown sugar. Put in quart jars and pressure-can according to manufacturer's directions.

# Venison Stew

**Serves 6–8**

*This is an original recipe I came up with to use my canned venison chunks. I have used beef chunks, but we preferred the venison over the beef. The recipe can be adjusted to the size of your family.*

*We really like venison meat, so we're always glad when my husband gets a deer or two. Then I like to always can some chunks, and of course some ground venison. Every year during deer season, my husband and his brothers go hunting, so we wives go along, too, and enjoy being there doing winter things such as sewing and making Christmas cards. And, of course, we cook food for our hungry men and listen to their deer stories. I'm glad they enjoy hunting and being out in the cold like that, because I'm glad for the meat they get.*

## INGREDIENTS

**1** quart venison chunks

**1** onion, sliced

**1** tablespoon butter

**1** quart broth or water

**2** cups potatoes, cubed

**2** cups carrots, sliced

**2** cups peas

**2** cups green beans, chopped

**¼** cup parsley, chopped

salt, pepper, and celery salt, to taste

## INSTRUCTIONS

Brown venison chunks and onion in butter until nicely browned. Add broth or water and the vegetables and seasonings. Cook until tender.

## Chilly Day Stew

**Serves 4–6**

### INGREDIENTS

**1** large carrot, chopped

**3** onions, chopped

**1** quart potatoes, peeled and diced

**2** tablespoons rice

**2** tablespoons macaroni

**1** teaspoon salt

water

**1** pint cream or milk

### INSTRUCTIONS

Bring a kettle of water to a rapid boil. Add carrot. While it is cooking, clean and chop 3 onions. Add them to the stew kettle. Add potatoes to the mixture. Add rice, macaroni, salt, and water to cover. Cook slowly until tender. When ready to serve, add cream or milk. Mix thoroughly but do not boil again. Serve with crackers or hot toast.

## Grandma's Broccoli Soup

**Makes 2 quarts**

### INGREDIENTS

**½** cup onion, chopped

**6** tablespoons butter

**6** tablespoons flour

**3** cups chicken broth

**2** cups milk

**4** cups (½ pound) fresh broccoli, chopped

**1** cup celery, chopped

**1** cup carrots, chopped

**1** tablespoon fresh parsley, minced

**1** teaspoon onion salt

**½** teaspoon garlic powder

### INSTRUCTIONS

Sauté onion in butter in soup pot until tender. Stir in flour to form a smooth paste. Gradually add broth and milk, stirring constantly. Bring to a boil and stir for 1 minute. Add vegetables and remaining ingredients. Reduce heat. Cover and simmer for 30–40 minutes, or until vegetables are tender.

# Cream of Potato Soup

**Serves 6**

*I remember when I was ten years old, there was a really bad snowstorm in our valley. School was cancelled for several days, which gave us a minivacation. We little girls worked on our embroidery patches and played with our dolls and games. But by midafternoon, we were bored and asked Mother what we could do. She told us we could make soup for supper and told us how to go about it. We added a little of this and a little of that and some leftovers and were amazed at how good it turned out!*

*Homemade soups are delicious, nourishing, and warming on a cold, wintry day—far better than any you can buy in cans. We often made some in the evening to put in our Thermos bottles for our school lunches. We felt sorry for those who had only dry sandwiches and pretzels in their lunch boxes.*

## INGREDIENTS

- **2** onions, chopped
- **2** ribs celery, chopped
- **4** medium potatoes, peeled and quartered
  boiling water
- **1½** teaspoon salt
- **¼** teaspoon pepper
- **2** tablespoons flour
- **3** tablespoons butter, softened
- **4** cups hot milk

## INSTRUCTIONS

Combine onions, celery, and potatoes in saucepan with a little water. Simmer until tender. Drain and reserve liquid. Mash cooked vegetables with potato masher. Add some reserved liquid and season with salt and pepper. Mash again. In a separate saucepan, blend flour with butter to a smooth paste over low heat. Add hot milk and remaining reserved onion/celery/potato cooking liquid. Bring to a boil, stirring constantly, until thickened. Add mashed potatoes, onions, and celery, and heat until steaming.

# Favorite Lentil Soup

**Makes 2 quarts**

*I am a teenaged Mennonite girl, the oldest of a family of ten, who likes to cook and bake. A while ago I got a bunch of used* Taste of Home *magazines from a lady I clean for. Oh, wow! What lovely, elegant dishes and exotic recipes! I pored over them every spare moment, longing to try them out. But unfortunately, almost every recipe called for something we didn't have on hand. I complained to my mother that all we had on hand were the basic staples, and that cooking the same old thing in the same old way was dull and boring. Mother looked pained, then went to have a consultation with Dad.*

*That very evening, he gathered us all together to tell us stories of when our forefathers were refugees and nearly starved to death. He said there are many starving people in the world yet today, and that we have no right to fare sumptuously every day (like the rich man in the Bible) while closing our eyes to the needs of these people.*

*Mother said if I want to try something new and different, I should try these lentil and barley recipes. They are family favorites now.*

## INGREDIENTS

**1½** cup lentils, rinsed and drained

**6** cups water

**2** slices bacon, diced

**1** medium onion, chopped

**2** carrots, thinly sliced

**2** ribs celery with leaves, sliced

**1** clove garlic, minced

**1½** teaspoon salt

**¼** teaspoon pepper

**½** teaspoon oregano

**1** (16-ounce) can whole tomatoes

**2** tablespoons lemon juice

## INSTRUCTIONS

Mix all ingredients together in a slow cooker and cook on low for 7–9 hours.

# Delicious Bean Soup

**Makes about 3 quarts**

*This bean soup is a prizewinner! At a local shop's Christmas banquet, it was in a twelve-quart kettle beside someone else's bean soup that was the main attraction. But theirs wasn't touched until our twelve-quart kettle was completely empty.*

## INGREDIENTS

- **1** pound dried navy beans, soaked overnight
- **1** tablespoon salt
- **1** onion, chopped
- **2** cups celery, chopped
- **½** cup butter
- **1** teaspoon garlic salt
- **2** tablespoons brown sugar
- **2** tablespoons molasses
- **½** pound bacon, fried and crumbled
- **½** pound cheese
- **1** cup tomato juice

## INSTRUCTIONS

Cook beans and salt in water until soft. Fry onion and celery in butter, and add to beans. Add rest of ingredients and heat. Mix and freeze in freezer boxes. When ready to eat, thaw and heat with a pinch of baking soda and milk, as desired.

# Chicken Corn Noodle Soup

**Makes about 12 quarts**

*This soup is a good seller at our benefit auctions, especially on cold days. It's also served at barn raisings and other get-togethers.*

## INGREDIENTS

- **4**  quarts water
-      chicken bouillon cubes or powder or flavoring, to taste
- **1**  pound kluski noodles
- **2**  quarts cooked chicken, diced
- **4**  quarts corn, fresh or frozen
- **1**  cup celery, finely diced
- **½**  cup onion, finely diced
- **½**  cup fresh parsley, chopped
-      black pepper, to taste

## INSTRUCTIONS

Bring water and chicken bouillon to boil. Add noodles and cook several minutes. Then add chicken, corn, celery, onion, parsley, and black pepper. Simmer until the noodles are done. Add more water if the soup becomes too thick. Taste to see if it needs more chicken flavoring or salt.

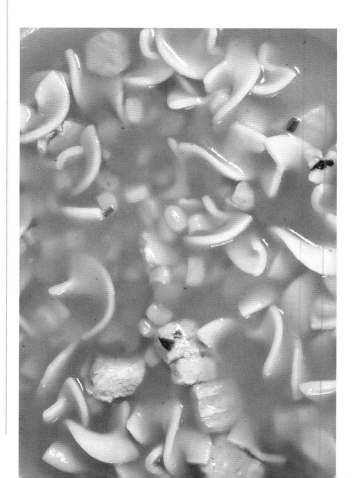

# Oven-Baked Stew

**Serves 8**

*On housecleaning days, I don't like to take time off to fix big meals, so it's usually soup or casseroles for us then. After a forenoon of sweeping, moving furniture, and scrubbing walls and floors, it's nice to have a hot meal ready in the oven for the family. When you're working hard, a meal of sandwiches and snacks doesn't hit the spot and isn't as filling.*

*A kettleful of bubbling cornmeal mush complements this one-dish meal. Our children like fresh things from our fall garden with it, too, such as sliced turnips, Chinese cabbage, and baby carrots.*

## INGREDIENTS

**2** pounds boneless, skinless chicken, cubed

**¼** cup flour

**¼** teaspoon celery seed

**1¼** teaspoon salt

**⅛** teaspoon pepper

**4** medium onions, sliced

**2** turnips, sliced

**1** cup celery, diced

**2** cups peas

**6** medium potatoes, thinly sliced

**2** medium carrots, thinly sliced

**1½** cup hot water

**4** teaspoons beef bouillon

**1** teaspoon Worcestershire sauce

  butter

## INSTRUCTIONS

Mix flour and seasonings and dredge meat in them. In a large casserole dish with tight-fitting cover, arrange in layers, meat and vegetables. Add bouillon to hot water and add Worcestershire sauce. Pour evenly over casserole. Dot with butter, cover, and bake at 325° for 3 hours.

## Easy Sloppy Joes

**Serves 8**

### INGREDIENTS

**2** pounds ground beef

¼ cup onion, minced

½ cup ketchup

**3** tablespoons brown sugar

**1** tablespoon vinegar

**1** teaspoon prepared mustard

**1** teaspoon Worcestershire sauce

**1** teaspoon salt

buns, for serving

### INSTRUCTIONS

Fry beef and onion. Drain. Add other ingredients and simmer 12 minutes. Serve warm on buns.

## Egg Salad

**Serves 4–6**

### INGREDIENTS

**6** hard-boiled eggs, mashed

½ cup mayonnaise

**2** tablespoons milk or cream

**1** tablespoon vinegar

salt and pepper, to taste

paprika, to taste

### INSTRUCTIONS

Mix ingredients together. Spread on bread.

# Hot Dog Boats

**Serves 8**

When we make this recipe, I think of the hot dog roast we had with our cousins in the middle of winter two years ago. The pond was frozen over solid, and our whole family (except Mom and the baby) decided to go skating that evening. The boys gathered plenty of firewood, and Dad made a big bonfire so we could keep warm while we rested. We wrapped potatoes in tinfoil and baked them in the fire, and roasted hot dogs on long, thin branches. We wrapped the hot dogs in homemade bread to eat them, because we had no rolls.

Dad let us skate as long as we wanted, and we made the most of it, staying until around ten o'clock. The weather wasn't as cold that night, as it was "windstill" (no wind) and hundreds of stars were twinkling overhead. We played tag and the boys played hockey at the other end of the pond. I hope we'll have good skating weather again this winter.

## INGREDIENTS

**8** hot dogs, diced

**1** cup cheese, diced

**1** teaspoon prepared mustard

**1** tablespoon ketchup

**1** tablespoon onion, minced

**1** tablespoon pickle relish

**8** hot dog buns

## INSTRUCTIONS

Mix all ingredients and fill 8 buns. Wrap in foil and bake 15 minutes or longer at 325°.

## Lucy's Kitchen Tip

To add nutrition to a peanut butter and jelly sandwich, sprinkle wheat germ over the peanut butter.

# Chicken Hoagies

**Serves 3**

*A few years ago we had a sub and bake sale to help with the hospital bills of a family in our community. The evening before, all the girls got together at our house to make the subs and wrap them. Many hands make light work, and we had a lot of fun chatting and visiting while making one thousand subs! They sold really well at the sale, and the baked goods went well, too. The family that got the proceeds could hardly believe it when we presented them with the check, and they said they felt almost too unworthy to accept it.*

### INGREDIENTS

**2** cups cooked chicken, diced
½ cup celery, diced
½ cup cheese, diced
**2** hard-boiled eggs, chopped
**2** tablespoons onion, minced
½ cup mayonnaise
  salt and pepper, to taste
  butter
**3** hoagie (long) buns
  tomato slices

### INSTRUCTIONS

Combine chicken, celery, cheese, eggs, onion, mayonnaise, salt, and pepper. Butter the buns, fill with chicken mixture, and wrap in foil. Heat in 400° oven for 20 minutes. Top with tomato slices.

# Hot Beef Subs

**Serves 6**

### INGREDIENTS

**1** pound ground beef
½ cup onion, chopped
**1** teaspoon salt
**1** (16-ounce) can baked beans
½ cup ketchup
**1** teaspoon prepared mustard
  processed cheese slices
  hoagie buns

### INSTRUCTIONS

Brown beef and onion. Add salt, baked beans, ketchup, and mustard. Stir and heat through. Spoon into hoagie buns and top with cheese slices.

# Popover Pizza

## Makes 1 (9 x 13-inch) pan

*One of the first times I made supper for our family, I was thirteen or fourteen and made Popover Pizza. But as it turned out, it came to be called "flop-over pizza."*

*The preparing part went okay, although the sink was rather splattered. I was rather "chicken" of the hot oven, so I timidly set the dish on the edge of the rack. But the bottom of the dish was wet, and it slid with a clatter and kersplash—down the open oven door, over the edge, down on the floor, and under the oven. Macaroni and meat and Bisquick over everything. The stuff on the door was sizzling already. What a mess!*

*By the time we got it all cleaned up, the men were in for supper and nothing was ready except some tomato soup. It was a while until I attempted to cook supper again. Right then I felt like crying and Mom was grouchy with me, but now we both laugh about it. I've made Popover Pizza several times and it is a quick, easy, filling main dish, and we love it.*

### INGREDIENTS

- **4** cups macaroni, cooked
- **1** (10¾-ounce can) cream of mushroom soup
- **1½** pound ground beef, browned
- **3** cups pizza sauce, divided
- **1** pound cheese, grated and divided
- **2** eggs, beaten
- **1** tablespoon oil
- **1** cup milk
- **1** cup Bisquick
- **2** tablespoons butter

### INSTRUCTIONS

Mix macaroni with cream of mushroom soup and set aside. Place ground beef in bottom of 9 x 13-inch pan. Top with half the pizza sauce and then half the cheese. Layer on macaroni mixture. Top with remaining pizza sauce and cheese. Mix together eggs, oil, milk, Bisquick, and butter to make crust. Pour carefully over casserole. Bake at 350° for 30 minutes, or until crust is golden brown.

## Lucy's Kitchen Tip

If your school children are tired of sandwiches in their lunch boxes, wrap pieces of pizza in tinfoil for them to heat on the school woodstove.

# Mom's Pizza

**Serves 8**

## INGREDIENTS

*Crust*

**2** tablespoons active dry yeast

**1** cup warm milk

**1** cup warm water

**¼** cup shortening

**1** tablespoon salt

**2** tablespoons sugar

**½** teaspoon oregano

**½** teaspoon thyme

**½** teaspoon garlic powder

**6** cups flour

*Toppings*

**3** pounds ground beef, browned

**2** medium onions, chopped

**2** (4-ounce) cans mushrooms

**2** quarts pizza sauce

**2** bell peppers, chopped

cheese, grated

hot sauce, optional

## INSTRUCTIONS

Mix yeast with milk and water. Stir in melted shortening. Stir in rest of ingredients and let rise 15 minutes in bowl, or until you have prepared filling. This crust makes a good herb bread–like crust with slightly crunchy edges. Spread crust out on two baking sheets. Mix ground beef and sauce and put on unbaked crust. Add toppings. Bake at 375° for 25–30 minutes.

# Veggie Pizza

**Serves 8**

## INGREDIENTS

*Dough*

**1** cup water

**½** cup butter

**1** cup flour

**4** eggs

*Spread*

**2** (8-ounce) packages cream cheese

**½** cup sour cream

**1** cup mayonnaise

**1** package dry ranch dressing mix

*Toppings*

raw, chopped vegetables of choice: lettuce, cauliflower, peppers, cucumbers, tomatoes, carrots, broccoli

cheese, grated

## INSTRUCTIONS

Mix water with butter in saucepan and bring to a boil. Add flour all at once. Stir rapidly until mixture forms a ball. Remove from heat and cool. Beat in eggs, one at a time, beating well. Spread on ungreased cookie sheet and bake at 400° for 30 minutes. Cool.

Mix spread ingredients. Spread over cooled crust. Sprinkle with raw, chopped veggies and grated cheese. Chill.

# Stromboli

**Serves 4–6**

*About five years ago, we used to farm produce. There was this one man who came for produce regularly and then sold it at his produce stand. He was a very big, hairy man, and he called himself "Fat Albert." We liked when he came because sometimes he brought us things. One especially yummy thing he brought along was stromboli. We thought that was such a treat.*

*Then over the years, my dad's back just got too bad to farm produce anymore, so he started an implement business, and since we stopped selling produce, of course Albert stopped coming, too. From then on, we started to make our own stromboli and we still make it and still love it!*

### INGREDIENTS

- **2** tablespoons active dry yeast
- **1** cup warm water
- **1** teaspoon sugar
- **2** tablespoons oil
- **1** teaspoon salt
- **2½** cups flour
  mayonnaise
  ham, sliced
  salami, sliced
  cheese, grated
  bell peppers, chopped
  onion, chopped

### INSTRUCTIONS

Dissolve yeast in warm water. Stir in sugar, oil, salt, and enough flour to make a medium-stiff dough. Knead well. Let dough rest 5 minutes. Roll out dough thinly. Spread with mayonnaise. Add ham, salami, cheese, peppers, and onion on half of dough. Fold rest of the dough over the top and seal sides. Let rise about 30 minutes. Bake at 400° for 20 minutes.

# Salads & Pickles

# Lettuce Bacon Salad

**Serves 4–6**

## INGREDIENTS

- **1** large head lettuce
- **1** large head cauliflower
- **1** small onion
- **2** cups mayonnaise
- **½** cup sugar
- **1⅓** cup Parmesan cheese, grated
- **1** pound bacon, finely cut and fried

## INSTRUCTIONS

Wash and cut up lettuce. Place in large bowl. Break up cauliflower into small pieces and put on lettuce. Add onions. Cover with mayonnaise. Sprinkle with sugar and then with cheese. Add bacon and cover. Set in refrigerator overnight. Mix well when ready to eat.

# Luscious Layered Salad

**Serves 8**

## INGREDIENTS

- **3** cups tomatoes, chopped
- **1** head lettuce, shredded
- **1** cup celery, diced
- **1** cup carrots, shredded
- **4** hard-boiled eggs, chopped
- **2** cups peas, slightly cooked
- **1** medium onion, chopped
- **8** slices bacon, fried and crumbled
- **2** cups mayonnaise or Miracle Whip
- **2** tablespoons sugar
- **4** ounces cheese, grated

## INSTRUCTIONS

In a 9 x 13-inch pan, make layers in order given: tomatoes, lettuce, celery, carrots, eggs, peas, onion, and bacon. Mix mayonnaise and sugar and spread on top. Top with cheese. Serve within 1 hour.

## Egg and Spinach Salad

**Serves 6**

### INGREDIENTS

- **6** hard-boiled eggs, chopped
- **5** cups spinach, chopped
- **6** slices fried bacon, crumbled
- **1** onion, minced
- **1** cup bean sprouts

*Dressing*
- **¾** cup sugar
- **¼** cup vinegar
- **¼** cup vegetable oil
- **⅓** cup ketchup
- **1** teaspoon salt
- **¼** teaspoon pepper
- **1** teaspoon Worcestershire sauce

### INSTRUCTIONS

Mix salad ingredients. Mix dressing. Toss salad with the dressing until spinach leaves are well coated.

### Lucy's Kitchen Tip

Save the water from hard-boiling eggs. Let it cool and then use it to water houseplants. Ferns especially like this and will turn greener.

## Red Beet and Apple Salad

**Serves 4**

### INGREDIENTS

- **2** cups cooked beets, diced
- **2** cups apples, diced
- **2** hard-boiled eggs, diced
- **½** cup celery, chopped
- **¼** cup nuts, chopped
- **¼** cup parsley, chopped
- **1** teaspoon vinegar
- **½** cup plain yogurt

### INSTRUCTIONS

Mix all together and serve on lettuce leaves.

# Lettuce Carrot Salad

**Serves 6**

*We think a meal is not complete without a good salad!*

*One year we had trouble with a bunny nibbling on our lettuce plants in the garden. We set a trap for it, but it was too smart for that.*

*When I mentioned to Daddy that something must be done about the rabbit in the garden, the four-year-old cried, "No! I won't let you hurt Peter Cottontail! I'm sure there's enough lettuce there for him and us both." At the time, his favorite bedtime story was about Peter Cottontail and Mr. MacGregor. He often sat out there beside the garden, hoping to get a glimpse of his friend Peter Cottontail.*

*Well, Daddy did get rid of the bunny, but he also bought two tame bunnies in a cage for our boy. Our son now happily feeds our extra loose-leaf lettuce to them.*

## INGREDIENTS

**1** head lettuce, chopped

**1** cup carrots, shredded

**2** cups cheese, shredded

*Dressing*

**2** cups sugar

**1** cup vinegar

**1** tablespoon mayonnaise

**½** cup cream

pinch salt

## INSTRUCTIONS

Place a layer of chopped lettuce on a flat dish. On that put a layer of shredded carrots. Top with shredded cheese. Mix dressing ingredients. When ready to serve, pour dressing over salad.

## Lucy's Kitchen Tip

Don't cut lettuce wedges unless you plan to use them within a few hours, as the edges have a tendency to turn brown. Tear the lettuce into portions, or use it leaf by leaf.

# Bacon Cauliflower Salad

**Serves 6–8**

### INGREDIENTS

- **1** pound bacon
- **1** head cauliflower, chopped
- **1** head broccoli, chopped
- **½** pound cheddar or Muenster cheese, shredded

*Dressing*
- **1** cup mayonnaise
- **¼** cup sour cream
- **1** package dry ranch dressing mix
- **½** cup sugar
- **½** teaspoon salt

### INSTRUCTIONS

Fry bacon and break into small pieces. Mix cauliflower, broccoli, and cheese with cooled bacon. Mix dressing and pour over salad.

# Easy Coleslaw

**Serves 6**

### INGREDIENTS

- **1** medium head cabbage, chopped or shredded
- **1** green bell pepper, finely diced
- **1** cup celery, chopped
- **1** small onion, finely chopped
- **2** teaspoons salt
- **1** teaspoon celery seed
- **1** teaspoon mustard seed
- **1½** cup sugar
- **½** cup white vinegar

### INSTRUCTIONS

Mix and refrigerate.

# Carrot and Celery Salad

**Serves 4–6**

*When I was a young girl, we had a dog that was fond of sweet things. He would sit up and beg nicely for treats and "shake-a-paw." We pampered him and fed him so many goodies that he grew quite fat. One day my older sister declared that this must be stopped. She bought a sack of lean dog food and forbade us to feed him anything but that. I pitied him so much and fed him whatever he wanted when Sis wasn't around.*

*Then one day he got sick and lost his appetite entirely. Since he was a valuable dog, we took him to a vet who gave him medication, which soon had him feeling better. The vet told us in plain words that there must be no more rich treats for doggie if we want him to stay well.*

*That should have taught me a lesson, but it seems I have to learn the hard way. I indulged too much, too, and now have to be on a reducing diet prescribed by my doctor. I'll include a few of my lean recipes here.*

### INGREDIENTS

- **4** medium carrots, shredded
- **¼** cup celery, finely chopped
- **1** tablespoon onion, finely chopped
- **2** tablespoons light mayonnaise
- **1** tablespoon sugar
- **2** tablespoons vinegar

### INSTRUCTIONS

Toss carrots, celery, and onion. Place in dish. Mix mayonnaise, sugar, and vinegar and pour over vegetables. This is best made 12 hours or more before serving.

# Sunshine Salad

**Serves 6**

### INGREDIENTS

- **1** (3-ounce) package orange gelatin
- **½** teaspoon salt
- **1½** cup boiling water
- **1** (8-ounce) can crushed pineapple
- **1** tablespoon lemon juice
- **1** cup carrots, grated
- **⅓** cup pecans, chopped

### INSTRUCTIONS

Dissolve gelatin and salt in boiling water. Add undrained pineapple and lemon juice. Chill until very thick. Fold in carrots and pecans.

## Garden Salad

**Serves 8**

### INGREDIENTS

½  cup celery, diced

½  cup carrots, diced

2  pints cooked peas

1–2 tablespoons onion, minced

2  hard-boiled eggs, chopped

½  cup cheese, diced or coarsely grated

*Dressing*

½  cup salad dressing

2  tablespoons sugar

1  tablespoon lemon juice or vinegar

1  teaspoon prepared mustard

### INSTRUCTIONS

Mix salad. Stir together dressing and mix into pea mixture. This refrigerates well.

## Three-Bean Salad

**Serves 6**

### INGREDIENTS

1  cup cooked navy beans

1  cup cooked red kidney beans

1  cup cooked string beans

4  hard-boiled eggs, chopped

1  large sour pickle, chopped

¼  cup onion, minced

3  tablespoons vinegar

1½ teaspoon salt

⅔  cup canola oil

### INSTRUCTIONS

Mix all together. Goes well with meat and mashed potatoes.

# Amish Macaroni Salad

**Serves 6**

*We like to go picnicking in the Wisconsin woods every fall, when the weather is golden and mellow and the sky is bright blue. Our favorite picnic spot is by the shallow creek, which is clear and flows over stones. There's a fire pit there and an old picnic table and benches in the shade. We think a picnic wouldn't be complete without either potato salad or macaroni salad, so I'll include our recipes for both.*

## INGREDIENTS

- **2** cups uncooked macaroni
- **½** cup celery, chopped
- **1** onion, chopped
- **1** teaspoon parsley
- **1** carrot, grated
- **6** hard-boiled eggs

*Dressing*

- **1½** cup sugar
- **¼** cup flour
- **¼** teaspoon salt
- **1½** cup water
- **½** cup vinegar
- **¼** cup mustard
- **1** cup mayonnaise
  celery seed, to taste

## INSTRUCTIONS

Cook macaroni as directed on package directions, and drain. Mix with remaining salad ingredients. Cook together sugar, flour, salt, water, and vinegar. Cool. Add mustard, mayonnaise, and celery seed. Stir into macaroni mixture.

# Deviled Eggs

**Makes 16 halves**

I am always hunting for new recipes to try, for cooking is one of my hobbies, and besides, variety is the spice of life. My brothers are glad that I try new dishes, judging by how fast things disappear, but they pretend that the food is terrible.

Once I unintentionally made a terrible dish, even though it wasn't a new recipe. We have a container of cayenne red pepper in the cupboard for when Grandpa comes. He always sprinkles it on his meat, saying it's good for his heart and circulation. Well, I made a platter of deviled eggs and accidentally (yes, it was accidental) sprinkled them liberally with Grandpa's red pepper instead of paprika!

The boys crammed the deviled eggs into their mouths and were soon sputtering and choking and running outside with water tumblers in hand. When I took a tiny nibble, I soon found out they weren't just playacting!

## INGREDIENTS

- **8** hard-boiled eggs
- **4** tablespoons mayonnaise
- **1** tablespoon cream
- **2** teaspoons vinegar
- **⅛** teaspoon pepper
- **½** teaspoon salt
- **½** teaspoon dry mustard
  paprika
- **2** tablespoons parsley, chopped

## INSTRUCTIONS

Cut eggs in half. Remove yolks, and mash them with mayonnaise, cream, vinegar, pepper, salt, and dry mustard. Refill the whites and sprinkle with paprika. Garnish with parsley.

# Anna's Potato Salad

**Serves 8**

INGREDIENTS

**12** medium-sized cooked potatoes, peeled and diced

**1** medium onion, finely chopped

**1** cup fresh parsley, finely chopped

**1½** cup mayonnaise

**1** cup cream

**¼** cup sugar

**¼** cup vinegar

**4** teaspoons mustard

**1** teaspoon salt

INSTRUCTIONS

Place potatoes, onion, and parsley in bowl. Mix rest of ingredients for dressing. Mix gently together. Refrigerate before serving.

# Ella's Zucchini Relish

**Makes about 10 pints**

INGREDIENTS

**10** cups zucchini, ground

**4** onions, chopped

**3** green bell peppers, chopped

**3** red bell peppers, chopped

**5** tablespoons salt

**6** cups sugar

**2½** cups vinegar

**2** tablespoons cornstarch

**2** teaspoons celery seed

**1** teaspoon mustard seed

**½** teaspoon powdered alum

INSTRUCTIONS

Mix salt into zucchini, onions, and peppers. Cover with water and let stand overnight. Drain well. Mix together remaining ingredients and stir into zucchini mixture. Simmer 30 minutes. Put into jars and seal according to manufacturer's directions. Delicious on hot dogs, hamburgers, eggs, and scrapple.

# Favorite Pickled Beets

**Makes 3–4 quarts**

*I'll never forget the day Mother and I were canning red beets last summer. I went to the garden with a knife to get a bucketful of golf ball–sized beets to rinse at the pump. I was daydreaming as I absentmindedly pulled the beets out and cut off the tops. Suddenly, right where I was reaching for a beet, I saw a spotted, curled-up snake! I screamed and leaped backward, and with two mighty jumps was out of the garden. My brother came running and killed the snake, and he had to get the rest of the red beets, too.*

## INGREDIENTS

- ½ gallon beets, small and young
- 2 cups sugar
- 2 cups water
- 2 cups apple cider vinegar
- 1 teaspoon cloves
- 1 teaspoon allspice
- 1 (1-inch) piece cinnamon stick
- 1 tablespoon salt

## INSTRUCTIONS

Cook beets until tender. Cool enough to slide off skins. Make syrup with remaining ingredients. Pour over beets and bring to a boil for 10 minutes. Pack in sterilized jars and seal according to manufacturer's directions.

# Hot Pepper Rings

**Makes about 1 gallon**

*Hot Pepper Rings is our favorite recipe for hot peppers. We got it from my cousin Becky. I remember so well when my little brother didn't know what Hot Pepper Rings were, and we told him to eat some. Oh my! Tears came to his eyes and he spit and spat, and actually cried. It took a while for the poor thing to eat them again. Once when he was sick with flu, he ate about a pint right out of the jar. He sure got better in a hurry! Also, eat them while hunting to keep warm.*

### INGREDIENTS

- **8** quarts hot peppers
- **1** quart vinegar
- **3** cups water
- **2** cups oil
- **⅓** cup salt
- **2** cloves garlic, minced and chopped
- **½** cup fresh oregano, chopped

### INSTRUCTIONS

Slice the peppers. (Wear rubber gloves to chop peppers or your hands will burn for hours.) Mix other ingredients together and pour over the peppers. Let stand at least 4 hours. Put in jars and waterbath for 5 minutes according to your canner's directions. Yummy if you like hot stuff!

# Dilly Pickled Green Beans

**Makes about 5 quarts**

### INGREDIENTS

- **2½** cups vinegar
- **2½** cups water
- **¼** cup salt
- **3** quarts green beans
- **4** cloves garlic, or **1** teaspoon garlic, minced
- **1** head dill weed, or **1** teaspoon dill seed

### INSTRUCTIONS

Boil vinegar, water, and salt together for brine. Remove ends of green beans; leave whole. Pack beans upright in wide-mouth quart jars, adding garlic and dill weed or dill seed to each jar. Seal according to manufacturer's directions.

# Pickles

**Makes about 4 quarts**

*A young girl who worked for me shared this recipe. She got it from an aunt. I tried this recipe and we really liked it. I'd serve it to company, and everyone who tasted these pickles wanted the recipe. I served them at a family picnic once, and everyone just loved them. Folks asked me many questions and wondered where I got such a good recipe. I've been copying this recipe for a lot of people.*

*My husband's aunt just recently told me she made lots of these pickles. She said she marked hers with first batch and second and third batch. Her family eats a lot of pickles, and she wants to use them in the order she made them. She was surprised when I told her she could keep them up to a year. So I keep sharing the recipe with others. This is the first time I had a recipe that everyone wants. I wonder how many I copied already!*

## INGREDIENTS

**5–10** cucumbers (each as long as a quart jar)

**2** cups vinegar

**1** cup water

**5** cups sugar

**1** teaspoon mustard seed

**1** teaspoon celery seed

**1** teaspoon turmeric

**1** teaspoon salt

## INSTRUCTIONS

Peel cucumbers. Slice lengthwise. Place in wide-mouth quart canning jars. Mix remaining ingredients. Fill jars. Seal jars according to manufacturer's directions.

# Bread and Butter Pickles

**Makes about 6 pints**

*I was having an extra busy day, with lots of pickles to can, laundry to do, and yard to mow. After dinner, I had a canner full of pickles ready on the stove in the shanty, intending to boil them for only a few minutes. After I put them on the stove, I stretched out on the kitchen couch to rest for a few minutes. I fell asleep and slept for about a half hour. When I awoke, I jumped up and looked guiltily at the clock. A thunderstorm seemed to be approaching, and I decided to quickly do some yard mowing before it rained. It wasn't until about an hour and a half later that I thought of my pickles. I rushed into the shanty, dreading to see what I'd find. The jars were okay, but the pickles were far from crisp anymore, needless to say! I suppose we'll be able to eat them, but I certainly won't be putting them on the table when we have company.*

*These are very crisp and crunchy, well worth the fuss, and not nearly as much time as the old fourteen-day sweet pickle.*

## INGREDIENTS

- **6** cups cucumbers, sliced
- **1** pound onions, chopped or thinly sliced
- **1** green bell pepper, chopped
- **¼** cup salt
- **2** cups brown or white sugar
- **2** cups vinegar
- **½** teaspoon turmeric
- **¼** teaspoon ground cloves
- **1** tablespoon mustard seed

## INSTRUCTIONS

Mix cucumbers, onion, and peppers with salt. Let stand 3 hours. Drain. Make a syrup with remaining ingredients. Bring to boil and add vegetable mixture. Put in jars and seal according to manufacturer's directions.

# Vegetables & Side Dishes

# Barbecued Green Beans

**Serves 8**

One summer evening my two daughters and I hitched the horse and drove to the neighbors to pick string beans. They had extra that year and we needed more, so they kindly offered to share with us. We tied the horse to the white barnyard fence and took our baskets to the garden.

We had already put two full baskets in the wagon and were starting to fill new baskets when we heard a clattering sound. Something must have scared the horse, and he tore loose and took off running home without us. The baskets upset, and there were beans scattered over the road. A neighbor man was coming down the road on a scooter and managed to stop the horse. We had enough beans left to can thirty quarts and make our favorite barbecued string beans.

### INGREDIENTS

**3** quarts green beans, cooked, salted, and drained

**1** onion, chopped

**1** cup ketchup

**1** cup brown sugar

**6** slices bacon

### INSTRUCTIONS

Put beans in baking dish. Mix onion, ketchup, and brown sugar and pour over beans. Bacon slices may be placed on top or chopped and mixed in. Cover. Bake at 275° for 4 hours.

# Baked Beans

**Serves 6**

### INGREDIENTS

**1** quart cooked beans with liquid

⅓ cup brown sugar

**2** tablespoons lard or shortening

¼ pound bacon, fried and crumbled

½ cup ketchup

salt and pepper, to taste

### INSTRUCTIONS

Mix and bake at 350° for 45 minutes, stirring a few times.

# Green Beans in Tomato Sauce

**Serves 8–10**

*Living in a new settlement with no church building yet, the people having the church services at their home would often invite the families to stay for dinner. When our turn came to have church at our house, I wracked my brain trying to think of something simple and easy to serve so there wouldn't be much work to do on a Sunday.*

*As I was trying to plan the menu, I thought about all the canned string beans and tomato juice we had in the cellar, and thought about making a sauce with the tomatoes, adding to it browned ground beef, and pouring it over string beans. That would do for the meat and the vegetable, and wouldn't need gravy. I could also make creamed potatoes to go with it and that would be a complete meal. So I devised my own recipe for the bean dish and hoped people would like it.*

*I was very surprised and pleased when, after our church meal was over, a proper Indiana lady asked me for the recipe of my meat and string bean dish. I had to tell her there was no recipe; I made it up myself! But I did try to write it out then, as I had made it.*

## INGREDIENTS

- **1** quart tomato juice
- **1** teaspoon salt
- **2** tablespoons sugar
  dash baking soda
- **1** tablespoon flour
- **2** tablespoons water
- **1** pound ground beef
- **1** small onion, chopped
  salt and pepper, to taste
- **2** quarts canned green beans, drained

## INSTRUCTIONS

Bring tomato juice, salt, sugar, and baking soda to a boil in saucepan. Mix water and flour to a paste and thicken. Brown the meat and onion in a frying pan. Season with salt and pepper. Drain and add to the tomato sauce. Pour sauce over canned green beans.

## Lucy's Kitchen Tip

Season your iron skillet to prevent food from sticking to the bottom and to keep the pan from rusting. Clean the skillet with hot water only, no soap. Heat it in the oven at 250° or on the stovetop until water evaporates. Rub fat or oil inside the hot, dry skillet. Repeat seasoning each time after you use the skillet.

## Two-Bean Bake

**Serves 6–8**

### INGREDIENTS

**2** cups cooked green string beans

**2** (15-ounce) cans kidney beans, drained

**1** medium onion, chopped

**½** cup ketchup

**3** tablespoons brown sugar

**1** cup celery, chopped

**2** tablespoons vinegar

**2** teaspoons mustard

**1** teaspoon salt

**4** slices bacon, fried

### INSTRUCTIONS

Combine beans and onion. Combine remaining ingredients, except bacon, and add to beans. Pour into baking dish and lay bacon on top. Bake at 375° for 45 minutes.

## Lima Bean Bake

**Serves 6**

### INGREDIENTS

**2** cups dried lima beans

**1** small onion, chopped

**1** green bell pepper, chopped

**1** cup canned tomatoes with juice

**2** teaspoons salt

**1** teaspoon dry mustard

**2** tablespoons brown sugar

**4** slices bacon, or 1 (2-inch) cube salt pork

### INSTRUCTIONS

Wash beans and soak overnight in cold water. In the morning drain and add 2 quarts fresh water. Cook until almost tender. Pour beans in a buttered casserole dish. Add onion, pepper, tomato, and seasoning and mix together. Place bacon or salt pork on top and bake, covered, for 1½ hour at 325°. Add more liquid if necessary. Remove lid and bake 30 more minutes.

# Easy Creamed Limas

**Serves 4–6**

*These lima bean recipes made me think of the pole limas we had in our garden when we were children. Four bean poles were set up like a teepee, and the beans climbed up these poles so vigorously that it formed a little playhouse inside. My sister and I took our little benches and sat inside the leafy house to play with our dolls, tell stories, or have a little snack. We had a litter of playful kittens and they liked to play there, too—pouncing on grasshoppers or playing tag with each other's tails.*

## INGREDIENTS

- **4** cups fresh lima beans
- **1** teaspoon sugar
- **2** teaspoons salt
- **2** tablespoons butter
- **⅛** teaspoon pepper
- **¾** cup milk
- **¼** cup cream
- **1** teaspoon cornstarch

## INSTRUCTIONS

Cook beans in water until tender and almost dry. Add seasoning, butter, milk, and cream. Bring to a boil and thicken with cornstarch.

# Carrot and Celery Bake

**Serves 6**

## INGREDIENTS

- **3** cups carrots, chopped
- **3** cups celery, cut into 1-inch slices
- **1½** cup cheese, shredded
- **1** (10¾-ounce) can cream of chicken soup
- **⅓** cup almonds, slivered or sliced
- **1** tablespoon butter or margarine

## INSTRUCTIONS

Cook carrots and celery in boiling water 8 minutes, then drain. Alternate layers of celery, carrots, cheese, and soup in a greased casserole dish, ending with soup. Lightly brown almonds in butter and sprinkle over top. Bake at 350° for 20–30 minutes, or until hot all the way through.

## Broccoli Bonanza

**Serves 8**

### INGREDIENTS

**2** (10-ounce) packages frozen chopped broccoli

**2** eggs

⅔ cup mayonnaise

**1** (10¾-ounce) can cream of mushroom soup

**1** medium onion, finely chopped

**1** cup cheese, grated

½ cup fine, dry bread crumbs

**2** tablespoons butter, melted

paprika

### INSTRUCTIONS

Cook broccoli according to package directions and drain well. Whisk eggs slightly. Add mayonnaise and soup and whisk to blend. Stir in broccoli, onion, and cheese. Turn into oblong 1½-quart baking dish. Mix bread crumbs and butter and sprinkle on top. Sprinkle with paprika. Bake in a preheated 350° oven approximately 35 minutes, or until sides begin to bubble.

## Favorite Scalloped Corn

**Serves 6**

### INGREDIENTS

**2** cups corn

⅔ cup cracker crumbs

½ teaspoon salt

⅛ teaspoon pepper

**1** tablespoon sugar

**1** teaspoon onion, minced

**1** cup milk

**2** eggs, beaten

**3** tablespoons butter, melted

### INSTRUCTIONS

Mix all together and pour into a greased casserole dish. Bake at 350° for 30 minutes.

# Onion Rings

**Serves 4**

*I'm a ten-year-old girl who likes to help Mom cook, and this is a simple recipe we love. Mom can't make these often enough to suit us! They're better than McDonald's or store-bought onion rings. It's so much fun to dip these onion rings and fry them.*

## INGREDIENTS

- ½ cup flour
- ¼ teaspoon salt
- ½ teaspoon baking powder
- 1 egg, lightly beaten
- 2 tablespoons oil
- ¼ cup milk
- 1–2 onions, cut into rings

## INSTRUCTIONS

Mix everything except for onions. Dip onions in mixture. Fry in hot oil, 365°. Drain onion rings on paper towels.

# Kansas Corn Pie

**Makes 1 (9-inch) pie**

*Years ago we had a pet raccoon that could open the screen door by himself and come into the kitchen whenever he wanted to. He knew he wasn't allowed up on the kitchen table, but we soon found out that if there were ears of fresh sweet corn on the table, he didn't have a conscience anymore, or else he forgot the rules! He looked so cute and comical when attacking a roasting ear that we couldn't help but laugh and laugh. We had an electric fence around our corn patch in the garden, so this was his only chance at his favorite snack.*

## INGREDIENTS

- **1¼** cup fine cracker crumbs
- **⅓** cup + **2** tablespoons butter, melted, divided
- **1¼** cup milk, divided
- **1½** cup fresh raw corn
- **½** teaspoon salt
- **2** tablespoons flour
- **½** teaspoon onion salt
- **2** eggs, beaten

## INSTRUCTIONS

Combine crumbs and ⅓ cup butter. Set aside ½ cup for topping. Line 9-inch pie pan with remaining crumbs. Combine 2 tablespoons melted butter, 1 cup milk, corn, and salt. Bring to boil; reduce heat and cook 3 minutes. Add flour to remaining ¼ cup milk and mix to smooth paste. Add slowly to corn, stirring constantly. Cook 2–3 minutes, or until thick. Cool slightly; add onion salt. Add eggs slowly, stirring constantly. Pour into crumb-lined pan. Sprinkle reserved crumbs on top. Bake 20 minutes at 400°.

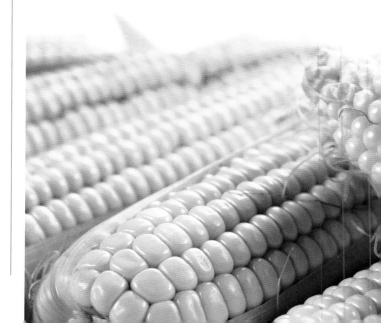

# Corn Croquettes

**Serves 6**

*One Sunday, when our parents were away visiting elderly friends, we children decided to have a "corn party" down at our picnic spot in the meadow. We made a campfire on our stone hearth with the old grate over top and boiled ears of corn in the old cast iron pot. We only had roasting ears to eat at our party, but they were about the most delicious we'd ever tasted. Maybe it was the flavor of the wood smoke or the tangy scent of the pines that did it.*

## INGREDIENTS

**2**  cups fresh corn

**2**  eggs

**1**  tablespoon butter, melted

**¼**  cup flour

**1**  teaspoon salt

**⅛**  teaspoon pepper

**1**  teaspoon baking powder

**1**  tablespoon cream

## INSTRUCTIONS

Mix all together. Drop by spoonfuls into hot fat in a frying pan and brown on both sides.

# California Potatoes

**Serves 6**

*During our first three years of marriage, we planted our own potatoes. But somehow we have never had enough to last through the winter. My sister-in-law shared potatoes with us so generously, but this spring we decided to make sure we'll have plenty. So we planted fifty pounds. Our friends and family thought we went to the other extreme! We planted the potatoes in the lowest part of the garden, not knowing, of course, that we'd have a very wet summer. God sent us many "showers of blessings" this summer, and we don't want to complain. We have plenty to eat but have even fewer potatoes for the winter than other years: they rotted in the wet ground! My kind sister-in-law is sharing potatoes again. She says she's glad to share and she knows we tried.*

## INGREDIENTS

- **6** medium potatoes
- **6** tablespoons butter or margarine, divided
- **1** (10¾-ounce) can cream of chicken soup
- **1** pint sour cream
- **⅓** cup onion, chopped
- **1½** cup cheese, shredded
- **2** cups cornflakes, crushed

## INSTRUCTIONS

Boil and slice potatoes, set aside. Heat 4 tablespoons butter or margarine and add undiluted soup, onion, sour cream, and cheese. Stir mixture into potatoes and place in a greased baking dish. Mix together cornflakes and 2 tablespoons melted butter. Place on top of potatoes. Bake at 350° for 45 minutes. Yummy!

# Party Potatoes

**Serves 4**

*On my fifteenth birthday, I was home alone for the day. Before the others had left for their various appointments, no one even mentioned my birthday. It was a very rainy day, but when the mail carrier went, I splashed through the downpour to see if a card had come for me. When none was there, I felt a bit forgotten and blue. I tried to do some sewing that afternoon, but after sewing a seam wrong and breaking two needles, I gave up in frustration. I didn't feel like cooking much for supper and decided that we'd all have to be satisfied with tomato soup. A little later a carriage drove in and it was my married sister, her husband, and baby. She had brought a complete supper for us, including party potatoes, baked beans, sauerkraut balls, and a birthday cake with candles for me. It turned out to be the best birthday I'd ever had!*

## INGREDIENTS

- **4** cups mashed potatoes
- **1** cup sour cream
- **1** (8-ounce) package cream cheese, softened
- **1** teaspoon dried chives or parsley flakes
- **¼** teaspoon garlic powder
- **¼** cup dry bread crumbs
- **1** tablespoon butter or margarine, melted
- **½** cup cheese, shredded

## INSTRUCTIONS

Mix potatoes, sour cream, cream cheese, chives, and garlic powder. Turn into a 2-quart casserole dish. Combine bread crumbs with butter. Sprinkle over potatoes. Bake at 350° for 50–60 minutes. Top with cheese and serve.

# Barb's Sweet Potatoes

**Serves 4**

### INGREDIENTS

- **3** cups cooked sweet potatoes, mashed
- **2** eggs, well beaten
- **½** cup sugar
- **⅔** cup butter, divided
- **1** cup brown sugar
- **½** cup flour
- **1** cup pecans, chopped
- **1** cup miniature marshmallows

### INSTRUCTIONS

Mix together sweet potatoes, eggs, sugar, and ⅓ cup butter. Place mixture in a greased casserole dish. Mix together remaining ⅓ cup butter, brown sugar, flour, and pecans. Crumble over top. Bake at 300° for 20–30 minutes. Arrange marshmallows on top and return to warm oven to melt and toast.

# Pineapple Sweet Potato Casserole

**Serves 4**

### INGREDIENTS

- **2** cups sweet potatoes, cubed
- **¼** cup cooked rice
- **1** (8-ounce) can pineapple with juice, chopped if necessary
- **1** tablespoon honey
- **1** tablespoon molasses
- **⅓** teaspoon salt

  marshmallows, optional

### INSTRUCTIONS

Mix and bake 1 hour at 350°. If desired, add marshmallows on top after baking and put back in oven to melt.

# Little Spätzlein

**Serves 4**

I remember the first time I tasted these Spätzlein. I was a little girl at Grandmother's house, where I stayed for a few days while my parents were visiting in Michigan. Because of their name, I thought they were boiled sparrows, and I didn't want to taste them at first. But my uncle really bragged them up and smacked his lips as he ate them to prove that they really were delicious. Finally I got up the courage to taste them, and to my surprise, they were quite good! I ate a big serving and later told my mother she ought to make them, too.

During that visit, Grandmother gave me a little butter plate with pink flowers on it, which I still have and value as a remembrance of her. Later we moved to another state and I didn't see my grandmother much anymore. My other grandparents weren't close by, so I don't have many memories of being at their house either. At least we could write to them and were thankful for the letters we received in return. I often think that the children who are privileged to grow up close to their grandparents really have a blessing.

## INGREDIENTS

- **1** egg, or **2** egg yolks
- **1** cup water
- **2½** cups flour
- **1½** teaspoon salt
- **¼** teaspoon turmeric
- **¼** teaspoon saffron threads
- **1** teaspoon dried parsley, optional
  dash black pepper
- **2** quarts boiling water
- **1** tablespoon butter

## INSTRUCTIONS

Beat the egg with a fork in a bowl, add 1 cup water, and continue beating until well blended. Work in the flour to make a soft batter. In a large kettle bring the seasonings, 2 quarts water, and butter to a boil. Tilt the bowl of batter over the kettle and cut with a spoon as it pours over, to make Spätzlein about 1 x ½ inch. Boil for 3 minutes after the batter is all in the water. Drain and top with plenty of browned butter.

# Noodles

**Serves about 6**

One winter day we were notified that school was cancelled for the day because something was wrong with the heater. Hurrah! Mother decided that since she had us girls at home to help, it would be a good day to make noodles. We mixed a double portion of dough, and soon our long table and the countertops were filled with rolled-out noodle dough, cut noodles, and noodles in various stages. We planned to eat dinner at the laundry room table, because the kitchen table was filled with noodles.

At eleven o'clock someone fetched the mail, and here was a card saying that our two uncles and aunts and their families—a whole vanload of them—were coming for dinner on Thursday. What? Thursday was today! A few minutes later the van was coming in the lane already! The postcard had been delayed for some reason, and we were unprepared.

The women pitched in and helped with the noodles, and the men and children patiently waited until the table was cleared. Everyone was satisfied with a meal of canned vegetable soup with plenty of fresh noodles in it.

## INGREDIENTS

- **6** egg yolks
- **6** tablespoons water
- **3** cups flour (approximately)
- **1** teaspoon salt

## INSTRUCTIONS

Beat egg yolks and water thoroughly. Work in flour and salt. Divide dough into 4 balls. Roll out very thin or put through noodle maker. Lay dough pieces separately in single layers on a cloth to dry. They're ready to cut when they're dry enough not to stick together; alternatively, iron dough with low iron on no-steam if you want them dry immediately. Cut into strips. Drop in boiling water and cook for 6–10 minutes. Store any dried, cut noodles in freezer to cook later.

## Noodle Cheese Bake

**Serves 6**

### INGREDIENTS

- **3** tablespoons margarine
- **8** ounces homemade noodles
- **½** pound processed cheese, sliced
- **1** teaspoon salt
- **¼** teaspoon black pepper
- **1** quart cold milk

### INSTRUCTIONS

Melt margarine in a 9 x 13-inch baking pan. Pour noodles in and stir until well coated. Cover with sliced cheese, each slice cut into fourths. Add salt, pepper, and milk. Bake, uncovered, at 325° for 1½ hour. Do not stir while baking. This comes out of the oven golden and creamy. Cold, sliced hot dogs and well-drained canned peas can be added.

## Noodles and Cheddar Cheese

**Serves 4–6**

### INGREDIENTS

- **2** cups uncooked noodles
- **2** cups cheddar cheese, shredded and divided
- **½** pound ground beef, browned
- **1** (10¾-ounce) can cream of mushroom soup
- **½** cup milk
- **½** cup canned tomatoes, chopped
- **¼** cup celery, chopped

### INSTRUCTIONS

Cook noodles in boiling, salted water until tender. Drain. In shallow baking dish, combine 1½ cup cheese with remaining ingredients. Top with ½ cup cheese. Bake at 350° for 30 minutes.

# Filling Balls

**Serves 8**

A few years ago, we were invited to our cousins' place nine miles away for our Thanksgiving dinner. When we woke up Thanksgiving morning, the ground was covered with several inches of snow, and it was still snowing. We were so disappointed to think of missing the gathering, so Dad borrowed the neighbors' two-seated sleigh and quickly reinforced and repaired it at some places. We put plenty of carriage blankets on the little ones and tucked them in up to their noses. I think I enjoyed that ride as much as I did the food, fun, and fellowship, for the snow was so beautiful with big flakes drifting down softly.

I got these filling recipes from my aunt, and they've been favorites of ours since.

## INGREDIENTS

**2** (20-ounce) loaves white bread, torn

**1** cup butter, melted

**1¼** teaspoon salt

**⅛** teaspoon pepper

**4** eggs, beaten

**2½** cups milk

## INSTRUCTIONS

Mix together in bowl. Shape into tennis ball–sized balls and arrange on baking sheets. Place in cold oven on upper rack. Turn oven on to 350° and bake for 20–25 minutes. Excellent topped with giblet gravy.

# Aunt Ida's Stuffing

**Serves 6**

## INGREDIENTS

**5** eggs

**1** quart milk

**1** teaspoon salt

**½** teaspoon pepper

**½** teaspoon poultry seasoning

**½** cup butter, melted

**1** cup celery, chopped

**½** cup onion, minced

**1** loaf bread, cut into cubes

## INSTRUCTIONS

Beat eggs well. Add remaining ingredients in order given. Pour into greased baking dish. Bake at 350°, covered, for 40 minutes, or until set. When almost done, uncover to brown top.

# Chicken Dressing

**Serves 8**

## INGREDIENTS

- **1** (20-ounce) loaf white bread
- **4** potatoes
- **1** carrot
- **1** small onion
- **1** rib celery with leaves
- **2** cups water
- **¼** cup chicken soup base
- **1** pint chicken broth and chicken pieces
- **3** cups milk
- **3** eggs, beaten
- **¼** cup butter, melted
- **¼** teaspoon poultry seasoning
- **¼** teaspoon black pepper

## INSTRUCTIONS

Toast bread and cube. Dice potatoes, carrot, onion, and celery. Cook in water and soup base until tender. When vegetables are done, mix with broth, milk, and bread cubes. Mix in eggs. Add butter and seasonings. Dressing should be moist. Place in greased 9 x 13-inch pan and bake at 400° for 45–60 minutes, or until firm and lightly browned.

## Lucy's Kitchen Tip

**Garden hint:** Plant your cabbage in the radish row. By the time the cabbage needs more room, the radishes are pulled for eating.

# Meats &
# Main Dishes

# Stormy Day One-Dish Meal

**Serves 4–6**

## INGREDIENTS

**1** quart carrots, sliced

**1** quart green beans

**3–4** potatoes, chopped

**1** quart canned beef chunks

**3–4** cups cabbage, chopped

**1–2** tablespoons flour

*Biscuits*

**2** cups flour

**½** teaspoon salt

**2** teaspoons sugar

**4** teaspoons baking powder

**½** teaspoon cream of tartar

**½** cup shortening

**⅔** cup milk

## INSTRUCTIONS

Mix carrots, beans, potatoes, and beef in large baking dish. Cover with cabbage. Cover with foil and bake in a moderate oven (350°) until vegetables are soft. Strain off broth. Whisk flour into it to thicken. Return thickened broth to baking dish. Make biscuits: Mix dry ingredients, cut in shortening, and stir in milk until a soft dough forms. Drop biscuits by spoonfuls on top of thickened broth and bake for 10–15 minutes more.

## Lucy's Kitchen Tip

In our grandmothers' time, herbs were used as medicinal teas more than in cooking. Experiment with thyme, marjoram, dill, and other herbs to add zest to simple, everyday meals.

# Baked Beef Casserole

**Serves 8**

## INGREDIENTS

¼ cup flour

¼ teaspoon celery seed

1¼ teaspoon salt

⅛ teaspoon pepper

2 pounds beef, cubed

4 medium onions, sliced

6 medium potatoes, thinly sliced

2 medium carrots, thinly sliced

1½ cup hot water

4 teaspoons beef bouillon

1 teaspoon Worcestershire sauce

   butter or margarine

## INSTRUCTIONS

Mix flour and seasonings and dredge beef cubes in them. In a large casserole dish with a tight-fitting cover, arrange meat and vegetables in layers. Add bouillon to hot water and add Worcestershire sauce. Pour evenly over casserole. Dot with butter. Cover and bake at 325° for 3 hours.

# Best-Ever Meatloaf

**Serves 6–8**

## INGREDIENTS

**2** eggs

**⅔** cup milk

**3** slices bread, torn

**1½–2** pounds ground beef

**½** cup onion, chopped

**½** cup carrot, grated

**1** cup cheese, shredded

**1** tablespoon fresh parsley, chopped, or 1 teaspoon dried

**1** teaspoon salt

**¼** teaspoon pepper

**1** teaspoon dried basil

**½** teaspoon red pepper flakes

*Topping*

**½** cup ketchup

**½** cup brown sugar

**1** teaspoon dry mustard

## INSTRUCTIONS

Beat eggs and add milk and bread. Let stand until bread has absorbed milk. Mix rest of ingredients with beef. Add bread mixture. Mix well and shape in a shallow pan. Mix topping and pour over all. Bake at 350° for about 1 hour.

# Seven-Layer Dinner

**Serves 6**

*We often serve this dish when we are busy working outside and haven't much time to prepare a full-course meal.*

*I put this in the oven a few days ago before we left for our back woodlot to pick up our shellbarks [hickory nuts]. We hitched Bob to the spring wagon and drove out the rutted back lane, enjoying the brightly colored leaves on the trees and the fall breezes and mists along the creek. The squirrels were busy gathering nuts, too, and scolded us aplenty for invading their territory. The two preschoolers each had their little sacks to fill, too.*

*I always enjoy this time of year when the summer harvest is in the barns and granary, and in jars on the cellar shelves. We have so much to be thankful for and must remember Whom to thank.*

## INGREDIENTS

**3** cups raw potatoes, sliced

**2** cups raw sweet potatoes, sliced

**2** cups celery, chopped

**½** cup onion, minced

**2** cups frozen peas, thawed

**1** pound ground beef, browned

**2** teaspoons salt

**¼** teaspoon pepper

**2** cups canned tomato juice

**1** cup water

**1** tablespoon butter

## INSTRUCTIONS

Place potatoes and sweet potatoes in bottom of greased casserole dish. Add celery, onions, peas, and ground beef. Sprinkle salt and pepper over all. Mix the tomato juice with water and pour over mixture in dish. Dot with butter. Bake at 350° for 2 hours.

## Lucy's Kitchen Tip

When youngsters are hungry and impatiently waiting for supper to be ready, give them carrot and celery sticks, broccoli florets, and the like. They'll eat more raw vegetables because they're hungry!

# Poor Man's Dinner

**Serves 6**

*I often make this one-dish meal when I'm in a hurry. We live on a farm—it's a quick dish for dinner or supper when we're busy outside, and it satisfies the hunger of the chore boys! I got the recipe from a lady I worked for as a hired girl, and now it's a favorite of our family and I pass it on to others.*

## INGREDIENTS

**1**    medium head cabbage

**1**    cup white rice

**2**    cups carrots, diced

**1**    quart raw potatoes, diced

**½**    cup onion, minced

**1**    tablespoon parsley, minced

**2**    teaspoons salt

**¼**    teaspoon pepper

**¼**    cup butter, melted

**1½** pound ground beef

**3**    cups tomato juice

**3**    cups water

## INSTRUCTIONS

Chop cabbage and put half of it in a greased roaster. Sprinkle rice over it. Add the carrots, potatoes, onion, parsley, and seasonings. Add the rest of the cabbage and melted butter, and spread ground beef over top. Pour tomato juice and water over all and bake at 350° for 2 hours or more.

## Note

Can use sausage instead of ground beef. It goes nicely with the cabbage.

# Vegetable Loaf

**Serves 4–6**

*This makes a nice one-dish meal; you have your meat and vegetables all in one, and it is handy and quick for a busy mother to mix up and put in the oven. It could also be served with noodles or elbow macaroni and a salad to go with it. Mmm!*

## INGREDIENTS

- **1½** pound ground beef
- **1** cup cabbage, chopped
- **1** cup potatoes, diced
- **1** cup carrots, diced
- **1** onion, finely chopped
- **1** cup bread crumbs
- **1** cup milk
- **1** egg
- **1** teaspoon salt
- **¼** teaspoon pepper
- **1** tablespoon butter, softened

## INSTRUCTIONS

Mix all ingredients together, as with meatloaf. Place in greased loaf pan. Bake at 350° for 2 hours.

### Note

Sometimes I like to put a glaze over the top made with ½ cup brown sugar, 1½ teaspoon prepared mustard, 1 tablespoon Worcestershire sauce, and 1 tablespoon vinegar. Spread over top and bake.

# Spinach Supreme

**Serves 6**

*I remember one snowy New Year's Day more than thirty years ago when my two sisters and I were home alone. We each decided to try out a recipe we'd never made before. We thought it was a very special meal, and I'll include three recipes we used (Spinach Supreme, below; Ham and Potatoes, page 137; and Barb's Sweet Potatoes, page 111).*

*That afternoon, we went for a walk in the snow along the creek that winds through the meadow. We tried to identify the tracks we saw of all the little woodland folks and birds. When we came back we felt famished again and polished off the leftovers! Whenever I feel twinges of homesickness for those long past days, I relive all the memories and make our special recipes again.*

## INGREDIENTS

- **2** pounds ground beef
- **2** eggs
- **¼** cup ketchup
- **¼** cup milk
- **¾** cup soft bread crumbs
- **1½** teaspoon salt, divided
- **¼** teaspoon pepper
- **¼** teaspoon dried oregano
- **1** (10-ounce) package frozen spinach, thawed
- **3** ounces smoked ham, sliced
- **3** slices mozzarella cheese, sliced diagonally into halves

## INSTRUCTIONS

Mix ground beef, eggs, ketchup, milk, bread crumbs, ½ teaspoon salt, pepper, and oregano. Pat into 10 x 12-inch rectangle on a piece of tinfoil. Arrange spinach evenly on top of meat, leaving a ½ inch margin around edge. Sprinkle with 1 teaspoon salt. Arrange ham on top. Carefully roll up, beginning at narrow end and using foil to lift meat. Press edges and ends of roll to seal. Place in ungreased 9 x 13-inch pan. Bake at 350° for 1 hour and 15 minutes. Overlap cheese triangles on roll. Bake 5 minutes more.

# Yummasetti

**Serves 8**

*My husband just loves this casserole. We were served this casserole when my in-laws came to see our new baby boy. (That was sixteen years ago.) We both liked it so much. Since then I have given recipes to friends who ate at our table. It's a full-course meal all in one dish.*

### INGREDIENTS

**1½** pound uncooked  noodles

**10** ounces bread (half a loaf), cubed

**2** tablespoons butter

**3** pounds ground beef

**1** onion, chopped

**2** (10¾-ounce) cans mushroom soup

**1** (10¾-ounce) can cream of chicken soup

**1** cup sour cream

**1** pint peas

### INSTRUCTIONS

Cook noodles in boiling salted water. Drain. Place in roasting pan. Toast bread in butter in frying pan. Place in roasting pan. Fry beef with onion. Drain. Place drained beef and onion in roasting pan. Mix the soups and sour cream together. Add to the other ingredients with peas. Mix gently. Bake, covered, for 1 hour at 350°.

### Note

I sometimes replace the canned soup with homemade white sauce.

# Stuffed Shell Casserole

**Serves 8**

*The first time I made this recipe was to serve my special friend for Sunday supper. He really liked it and has asked me to make this many times since we are married. I always make it for his birthday in the summer and our anniversary in the fall, and many times in between. Our children like it too and they'll occasionally ask me to make "seashells"! We've tried other stuffed shell recipes, but never have we had any as good as this one.*

## INGREDIENTS

- **1** egg
- **¾** cup bread crumbs
- **1** tablespoon onion, chopped
- **½** teaspoon salt
- **1** pound ground beef
- **2** cups mozzarella cheese, shredded and divided
- **15** jumbo shells, cooked according to directions on box

*Sauce*

- **1** quart tomato juice
- **¾** cup brown sugar
- **¼** teaspoon salt
- **1** tablespoon oregano
- **1** tablespoon Clear Jel

## INSTRUCTIONS

Combine egg, bread crumbs, onion, salt, beef, and 1½ cup mozzarella. Stuff in shells.

Bring sauce ingredients to a boil and thicken with Clear Jel to consistency of gravy. Pour half of sauce into 9 x 13-inch baking pan. Place stuffed shells in sauce. Pour other half of sauce over top. Sprinkle with the last ½ cup of shredded cheese. Cover and bake in slow oven for 2 hours at 325°.

# Burrito Casserole

**Serves 4–6**

Some years ago my younger brother broke his leg. He had been an active outdoor boy and was often bored, sitting there with not much to do while his leg healed. We were all very busy helping with the produce, so I decided to get him interested in helping with the cooking. I told him that his future wife would be very pleased if he could give her a helping hand when necessary. He did take an interest in it, and soon he was learning to follow recipes and stir together the dishes he liked, making changes here and there to suit his fancy. He was never much for desserts and baked goods, so he chose casseroles and main dishes for his projects.

I copied some of his favorite ones into a small booklet and illustrated it. I wrote "Dan's Own Cookbook" on the cover and gave it to him for Christmas. Just recently I asked his wife if he still has it and she said, "Yes, indeed. He cherishes it, too, and those dishes are still among his favorites." Maybe when this cookbook is finished, I can give him a copy of it, too, with his recipes in it.

## INGREDIENTS

**1–1½** pound ground beef

**1** onion, chopped

**1** (16-ounce) can refried beans

**1** package taco seasoning

**16** ounces sour cream

**1** (10¾-ounce) can cream of mushroom soup

**8** (8-inch) tortillas

**4** cups cheese, shredded

## INSTRUCTIONS

Brown meat and onion. Add taco seasoning and beans. Mix sour cream and soup together. Put some in bottom of 9 x 13-inch pan. Put ½ cup meat mixture in each tortilla and roll up. Place seam-side down in soup mixture in pan. Spread remaining soup mixture on top of tortillas and top with cheese. Bake at 350° for 30 minutes, or until cheese is melted and burritos are hot. Serve with lettuce, tomato, and taco sauce.

# Beef Noodle Casserole

**Serves 6–8**

*Ascension Day is usually the day our family gets together for a picnic if the weather permits. What better way to enjoy God's creation than to walk along nature's trails and see the beauties of his handiwork?*

*I am always reminded to bring this dish (my specialty), and so far I've never had to carry any back home again. After the plates, cups, and empty dishes are repacked into the baskets, we women sit in a circle and visit, and the young fry run off to explore the woods and meadows.*

*Sometimes we stay for supper, too, and I am reminded of the song: "Come Home—It's Suppertime. . . . It's Suppertime upon That Golden Shore."*

## INGREDIENTS

- **1** pound uncooked noodles
- **4** teaspoons salt, divided
- **4** pounds ground beef
- **¼** teaspoon pepper
- **1** cup onion, chopped
- **2** cups cooked corn
- **1** pound cheese, grated

*White Sauce*
- **½** cup butter
- **½** cup flour
- **1** tablespoon salt
- **6** cups milk

## INSTRUCTIONS

Boil noodles in 2 quarts boiling water and 2 teaspoons salt. Brown the beef with 2 teaspoons salt, pepper, and onion. Drain off fat and set beef aside. Make white sauce: Melt the butter in a heavy saucepan. Add flour and salt and stir until well blended. Slowly add the milk, stirring and simmering until thick. In a big casserole dish or roasting pan, layer half the noodles, half the corn, half the beef, half the white sauce, and half the cheese. Repeat layers. Bake at 350° for 1 hour.

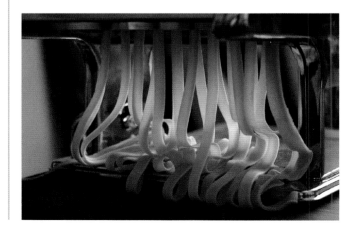

# Beef and Cheese Casserole

**Serves 4–6**

*Our first baby was so fussy that my husband and I took turns walking the floor with him, sometimes night and day. Kind neighbors and friends sent in casseroles and soups and even complete meals. When he was three months old, his colic mysteriously disappeared and he became a contented baby. What a blessed relief and joy!*

*I got some of the recipes from those who had sent meals and will share one of them here. I wouldn't want to live those hard weeks over again, but it was a learning experience, too. It taught me to try and help others more when they are in need and to really appreciate our baby's sunny smiles and contented cooing.*

## INGREDIENTS

**8–10** potatoes, boiled

¼ pound dried beef

**2** tablespoons butter

**2** tablespoons flour

**2** cups milk

**1** cup cheese, any kind

**2** tablespoons bread crumbs, buttered

¼ cup parsley, chopped

## INSTRUCTIONS

Slice half of the potatoes into a 2½-quart casserole dish. Fry beef slightly in butter. Add flour and mix well. Add milk and cheese. Cook until thickened. Pour half of sauce over the potatoes. Add remaining potatoes, then the rest of the sauce. Sprinkle bread crumbs on top. Bake at 350° for 30 minutes. Garnish with parsley.

# Macaroni Casserole

**Serves 8–10**

*I am the fourth girl in a family of seven children. My two oldest sisters are married. We often served this delicious casserole when their boyfriends came for supper. It's easy to make, and best of all, everyone likes it. Enjoy!*

## INGREDIENTS

- **4** cups uncooked macaroni
- **3** cups cooked peas
- **1** pound any kind of meat, cubed
- **1** pound processed cheese, cubed
- **2** cups milk
- **2** (10¾-ounce) cans cream of chicken soup
- **2** teaspoons salt

## INSTRUCTIONS

Cook macaroni and drain. Add peas and meat. Simmer processed cheese, milk, soup, and salt until cheese is melted. Add to macaroni. Place in greased casserole dish. Bake at 300° for 1 hour.

*Note*

For Sunday dinner, bring macaroni and peas to boiling, drain, and add other ingredients. Bake at 250° for 3 hours.

# Pizza Casserole

**Serves 4–6**

*This is my favorite pizza casserole recipe, and the whole family enjoys it. We got it out of our weekly newspaper. It is a joy for me to try out new recipes, so when we receive our newspaper that has recipes in it, the first thing for me to do is check if there is a good, simple recipe.*

*One of my friends was sick and had to be in the hospital for a few days. We put some quilt tops together and made a few quiltings for them in hopes that the quilts would sell to help them pay their hospital bill. We also planned a quilting at their house, so we decided to furnish a pizza casserole like this for lunch. At least one lady asked for the recipe. They thought it was so delicious!*

## INGREDIENTS

1⅓ cup flour

2  teaspoons baking powder

⅔  teaspoon salt

¼  cup oil

½  cup milk

½  cup uncooked macaroni

2  pounds ground beef

1  onion, diced

2  cups pizza sauce

1  cup sour cream

3  cups cheese, grated

## INSTRUCTIONS

Mix flour, baking powder, salt, oil, and milk. Press into bottom of 9 x 13-inch pan. Cook macaroni and drain. Fry together ground beef and onion. Mix with macaroni and pizza sauce. Put mixture on the unbaked crust. Mix sour cream and cheese and put on top. Bake at 350° approximately 1 hour.

# Party Pizza Casserole

**Serves 4–6**

We are a family of eight who live on an eighty-acre dairy farm. We all like this dish—especially our farm dogs! Let me tell you how we know.

One evening in July, we were planning to eat down by the Conestoga River, which flows through our meadow. We have a picnic table and a fireplace there in a grassy, shady spot that we keep mowed. My older brother went down first to start the campfire, taking the hot casserole along and setting it on the picnic table. A short while later, he came back for the hot dogs, and soon all of us were ready to go too. Dad decided we'd better hitch the horse to the spring wagon, and the younger children piled on back and we started off.

When we arrived at the campfire, two very guilty-looking dogs were slinking shamefacedly away. They had knocked the lid off the casserole and eaten some of it. I hope they burned their tongues good and proper!

## INGREDIENTS

- **2** pounds ground beef
- **1** green bell pepper, chopped
- **1** red bell pepper, chopped
- **1** pint pizza sauce
- **8** ounces sour cream
- **1** (1-ounce) package onion soup mix
- **3** (16-ounce) cans biscuits
- **2** cups mozzarella cheese, shredded

## INSTRUCTIONS

Brown ground beef and peppers. Add pizza sauce, sour cream, and onion soup mix. Set aside. Bake the biscuits according to directions on can. Place over the bottom of a big baking pan. Layer meat and cheese mixture over it. Bake at 350° just long enough to heat throughout.

# Lisa's Lasagna

**Serves 6**

*I got this recipe from a friend of mine who hosted a mystery dinner one Sunday. We girls were all seated at the table, but there was no food or plates or utensils on it. We each got a list and could choose three items from it. Some of the things listed were Shimmering Silk, Mountain Sauce, Tangled Topiary, Dazzling Delight, Sculptor's Scheme, and Splendid Creation. I don't remember the rest, but for most of them, we hadn't a clue as to what we were ordering.*

*One girl got a chocolate cupcake, a mound of mashed potatoes, and a pickle with no utensils! She ate the mashed potatoes with her pickle! I was lucky; I got lasagna, potato salad, and a fork. For my next course, I got ice cream dessert, apricot jam, and a knife!*

*The lasagna was the Splendid Creation, and I liked it so well that I copied off the recipe.*

## INGREDIENTS

- **1** pound ground beef
- **4** cups spaghetti sauce
- **10** ounces lasagna noodles
- **2** eggs
- **8** ounces cottage cheese
- **½** cup Parmesan cheese, grated
- **2** tablespoons parsley flakes
- **1** teaspoon salt
- **½** teaspoon pepper
- **1** pound mozzarella cheese

## INSTRUCTIONS

Brown meat and drain fat. Add sauce. Cook noodles and drain. Beat eggs. Add cottage cheese, Parmesan cheese, parsley, salt, and pepper. Make layers in a 9 x 13-inch pan: a third of noodles, a third of the cottage cheese mixture, a third of the meat sauce. Repeat layers twice more, sprinkling mozzarella on top. Bake at 375° for 45 minutes.

# Barbecued Meatballs

**Makes 60 small meatballs**

*"These meatballs are delicious!" I exclaimed as I tasted a crumb. I was one of the cooks at a wedding where they were having them for dinner. The two stoves standing side by side had their ovens full with cake pans of meatballs. All forenoon the delicious aroma kept tempting us. Just before noon, the head cook began checking them for doneness, taking a meatball from the center of each pan. We each had a bite. How delicious! When the time came to plan who would dish up what, we all jumped for the meatballs.*

*For the first sitting we carefully placed only the nice ones on the platters, nibbling on the broken pieces. The second sitting likewise. We kept chiding each other about picking at the meatballs. Some commented on how hungry they were getting and how good those meatballs will taste with mashed potatoes, salad, and so forth.*

*While filling the platters for the third and last sitting, someone remarked that there weren't a lot left anymore. The table waitresses were asked how many people were to eat at this last sitting. We counted the meatballs and discovered there just might not be enough, especially if some of the men took two.*

*Sure enough, by the time the cooks sat down to eat (we were last to be served), there were only crumbs and sauce left on the platters! Thank goodness I got the recipe.*

## INGREDIENTS

- **6** pounds ground beef
- **2** cups quick oats
- **4** eggs
- **2** cups cracker crumbs
- **4** teaspoons salt
- **¼** teaspoon pepper
- **½** teaspoon garlic powder
- **2** small onions, chopped
- **2** cups evaporated milk

*Sauce*
- **4** cups ketchup
- **2** teaspoons liquid smoke
- **2** cups brown sugar
- **½** teaspoon garlic powder
- **½** cup onion, chopped

## INSTRUCTIONS

Shape into balls. Place in shallow layer in baking pans. Mix sauce ingredients. Pour sauce over balls. Bake, uncovered, at 225° for 1–2 hours, stirring once or twice.

# Bacon Beef Balls

**Serves 4**

## INGREDIENTS

**3** slices cooked bacon, crumbled
**½** cup uncooked rice
**½** cup water
**⅓** cup onion, chopped
**1** teaspoon salt
**½** teaspoon celery salt
**⅛** teaspoon pepper
**⅛** teaspoon garlic powder
**1** pound ground beef
**2** tablespoons cooking oil
**2** cups tomato juice
**2** tablespoons brown sugar
**2** teaspoons Worcestershire sauce

## INSTRUCTIONS

Combine bacon, rice, water, onion, salt, celery salt, pepper, and garlic powder. Add beef and mix well. Shape into 1½-inch balls. In a large skillet, brown meatballs in oil. Drain. Combine tomato juice, sugar, and Worcestershire sauce. Pour over meatballs. Reduce heat. Cover and simmer 1 hour, or bake for 1 hour at 350°.

# Ham and Potatoes

**Serves 6**

## INGREDIENTS

**½** pound smoked ham
**6** large potatoes, sliced
**1** teaspoon salt
**1½** teaspoon flour
**½** cup thin cream

## INSTRUCTIONS

Cut ham into small cubes and cook until almost tender. Then add sliced potatoes and salt. When potatoes are soft and almost dry, whisk together flour and cream and add to potato mixture. Cook until thickened, and serve.

# Ham, Cheese, and Broccoli Bake

**Serves 6**

I don't think we'll ever forget the first time we tried out this recipe! Our daughter had invited her special friend, who lived in another state, to our home as guest at a Sunday evening meal. She was anxious to have everything shipshape and the food tasty and appealing. "First impressions are so important," she declared. "I just wonder what he will think of my family, our home, and the meal."

"It's you he is interested in, and he probably won't notice what he's eating," I teased. "Just relax and be yourself." But she was determined to have everything tip-top.

She had gotten this delicious-sounding recipe from a friend and wanted to try it out for this special occasion. It turned out beautifully! To add a decorative touch she garnished it with sprigs of parsley and halved cherry tomatoes around the rim. Everything went as planned until it was time to serve her fancy dish.

As she was carrying it to the table, it somehow slipped out of her hands and flopped upside down on the floor! She was terribly embarrassed and disappointed and later said she was close to tears, sure that her boyfriend would think her awkward and doppich (clumsy). But apparently he didn't. That very evening he asked for her hand in marriage, and they chose a wedding date.

## INGREDIENTS

**12** slices frozen bread

**6** slices bacon, fried and crumbled

**1** pound cheese, grated

**20** ounces frozen broccoli

**4** cups ham, diced

**10** eggs

**7** cups milk

**4** teaspoons dried onion, minced

**1** teaspoon salt

**½** teaspoon dry mustard

processed cheese, sliced

## INSTRUCTIONS

Layer bread, bacon, cheese, broccoli, and ham in a 9 x 13-inch pan. Beat eggs; add milk, onion, salt, and dry mustard. Pour milk and egg mixture over all. Refrigerate 6 hours. Bake at 325° for 1 hour. Lay cheese slices on top and allow to melt before serving.

# Holiday Ham Casserole

**Serves 4–6**

*I am an Amish girl, age sixteen, who likes to cook and try new recipes. My six brothers tease me about trying to make guinea pigs out of them, but I notice that they usually have a hearty appetite for anything I make.*

*The first time I made this recipe, my fourteen-year-old brother decided to play a trick on me. The table was all set with the big, double-portion casserole on hot pads in the middle. While I was out at the bulk tank in the milk house for a pitcher of milk, he sneaked into the kitchen and sliced some raw turnips (which I loathe) and stuck them here and there into the casserole, then ran outside again. I knew right away from his guilty face that he must have done something, but thought he'd just been sneaking a few bites. He just wanted to watch my face when I bit into a turnip slice while eating!*

*Well, I got even with him later. But that's another story.*

## INGREDIENTS

- **2** (10¾-ounce) cans cream of mushroom soup
- **2** cups milk
- **1** tablespoon green bell pepper, chopped
- **2** tablespoons onion, minced
- **1** tablespoon parsley, chopped
- **¼** teaspoon black pepper
  salt, to taste
- **½** pound processed cheese
- **4** cups cooked macaroni
- **2** pounds cooked ham, cubed

## INSTRUCTIONS

Combine soup, milk, pepper, onion, parsley, pepper, and salt. Place over low heat. Add cheese and stir until melted. Mix macaroni with the cheese sauce. Pour half of this in a 1½-quart casserole dish. Cover with half the ham cubes. Add remaining macaroni and sauce. Top with the rest of the ham. Bake at 325° for 30 minutes.

# Creamy Chicken and Rice

**Serves 4–6**

*With a new baby in the house, who is very* brauf *(good) and sleeps almost from one feeding to the next, I believe I'll have time to copy a few recipes and comments.*

*She was born on my birthday, and the next evening our neighbors sent over a full-course meal for supper, including a decorated birthday cake. How thoughtful! It certainly is nice to have good neighbors. I later got my neighbor's chicken recipe, which we thought was simply delicious and which I intend to make often. We have around thirty broilers, which will be ready to butcher soon with the help of my sisters.*

## INGREDIENTS

- ¼ cup onion, finely chopped
- ¼ cup celery, finely chopped
- ¼ cup butter
- 1 (10¾-ounce) can cream of chicken soup
- 1 (10¾-ounce) can cream of mushroom soup
- 3 cups cooked chicken or turkey, chopped
- 1 cup uncooked long-grain rice
- ½ teaspoon poultry seasoning
- 1 teaspoon salt
- 2 cups milk
- 2 cups chicken broth

## INSTRUCTIONS

Sauté onion and celery in butter. Add all other ingredients and mix well. Bake in 9 x 13-inch pan, uncovered, for 2 hours at 325°. Stir occasionally.

## Crisp and Tender Chicken

**Serves 4–5**

### INGREDIENTS

- **1** cup flour
- **1** tablespoon salt
- **½** teaspoon seasoned salt
- **¼** teaspoon pepper
- **1½** tablespoon paprika
- **1** frying chicken, cut up
- **2** tablespoons butter, melted
- **2** tablespoons milk

### INSTRUCTIONS

Combine flour, salt, seasoned salt, pepper, and paprika. Work mixture into chicken pieces, leaving no moist spots. Brown chicken in a ½ inch of hot fat, then place single layer in baking pan. Drizzle melted butter and milk over pieces. Bake, uncovered, at 350° for 30–40 minutes, or until tender. Pour extra milk over chicken during baking if chicken looks dry.

## Oven-Baked Chicken

**Serves 6–8**

### INGREDIENTS

- **2** frying chickens, cut into serving-sized pieces
- **½** cup butter, melted
- **2** teaspoons salt
- **1½** cup cornflakes, crushed
- **¼** cup Parmesan cheese, grated
- **¼** teaspoon pepper

### INSTRUCTIONS

Dip chicken pieces into butter, then in mixture of remaining ingredients. Arrange in two 9 x 13-inch baking dishes, allowing space between pieces. Bake, uncovered, at 350° for 1½ hour, or until tender.

**Variation:** Brush chicken with ¾ cup mayonnaise instead of melted butter, and increase Parmesan cheese to ½ cup.

# Huntington Chicken

**Serves 8–10**

*Once we decided to kill the rest of our chicken flock to can for the winter. We were almost done when to our surprise, one lone rooster strutted by. By all appearances, he realized how lucky he was to have slipped past unseen! So we decided to let him go for the moment and enjoy a roast later.*

## INGREDIENTS

- **8** tablespoons flour
- **¾–1** cup milk
- **1** tablespoon poultry seasoning
  salt and pepper, to taste
- **4** cups chicken broth
- **1** cup cheese, grated
- **1** cooked hen, boned
- **2** cups cooked macaroni, drained
  bread crumbs, buttered

## INSTRUCTIONS

Combine flour, milk, and seasonings. Stir mixture into broth and heat, stirring until thick. Melt cheese into the gravy. Pour over chicken and macaroni. Do not overstir or meat will get stringy. Pour into casserole dish and top with buttered bread crumbs. Bake at 350° for 30 minutes, or until bubbly.

# Make-Ahead Casserole

**Serves 8**

*Greetings from Ohio. We live on a thirty-three-acre produce farm and have six daughters and four sons. This casserole came in very handy during our busy season, when we're sometimes out in the fields picking produce from dawn to high noon. Fresh berries and vegetables must be picked when they're ready, and this makes for very busy spurts.*

*We enjoy it, but are thankful when the busy season is over and we can relax more and enjoy a slower pace. Our eleven-year-old son, Dan, broke his leg one summer, and he learned to get simple meals on the table when we womenfolk were too much on the run. I think one of our girls made a small cookbook for him of easy recipes and hints. We try to make up for those hectic times later by cooking more elaborate and extra-special meals.*

## INGREDIENTS

- **4** cups uncooked seashell macaroni
- **4** cups cooked chicken, cubed
- **2** (10¾-ounce) cans cream of mushroom soup
- **2** (10¾-ounce) cans cream of chicken soup
- **½** pound cheese, shredded
- **2** cups milk
- **½** cup onion, minced
- **¼** cup butter

## INSTRUCTIONS

In the morning, mix all ingredients well and put in a roaster. Refrigerate until you are ready to bake. Bake at 350° for 1 hour. Serve with a large lettuce and tomato salad.

# Aunt Anna's Chicken Casserole

**Serves 20**

*My husband used to go with the neighborhood silo-fillers when he was a teenager. It was a job he enjoyed, even though it had its dangers. He liked the good meals he got at the places where they were filling and even remembers some of the dishes they were served. One of them was this casserole, and I later got the recipe from the lady of the house. I make it often now, and his eyes light up when he sees it on the table.*

*I'm always glad when the silo-filling and harvesting season is over, and the fields are ready for the winter snows. We neighbors get together for a carry-in dinner every fall after the harvest, and I usually bring this casserole.*

### INGREDIENTS

- **12** cups bread cubes
- **12** cups cooked chicken, chopped
- **12** tablespoons parsley or celery leaves
- **6** teaspoons pepper
- **12** eggs
- **8** cups milk
- **8** cups chicken broth

### INSTRUCTIONS

Place a layer of bread cubes in a greased roasting pan, then add a layer of chicken, parsley, and seasonings. Continue in alternate layers, ending with bread cubes on top. Beat eggs and add milk and broth. Pour over mixture. Bake at 350° for 1 hour.

# Creamed Chicken

**Serves 8**

*Our family never gets tired of Creamed Chicken. We have it every Saturday evening for supper.*

## INGREDIENTS

**1** cooked chicken, deboned to equal 2 quarts chicken pieces with broth

**3** cups uncooked macaroni

**2** (10¾-ounce) cans cream of chicken soup

**2** (10¾-ounce) cans cream of celery soup

**2** (12-ounce) packages frozen peas

**2** cups processed cheese, cubed

**1** onion, chopped

**2** cups bread crumbs

**¼** cup butter, melted

## INSTRUCTIONS

Cook macaroni in chicken broth. Stir in soups, peas, cheese, and onion. Placed in greased casserole dish. Mix bread crumbs and melted butter. Sprinkle on top. Bake at 350° for 1 hour. Delicious!

# Hot Chicken Salad

**Serves 4**

*We like this salad with a meal of mashed potatoes, noodles, and peas.*

## INGREDIENTS

**1** cup celery, diced

**2–3** cups cooked chicken, chopped

**1** (10¾-ounce) can cream of chicken soup

**2–3** hard-boiled eggs, chopped

**1** teaspoon onion, minced

**1** cup cooked rice

**¾** cup mayonnaise

salt and pepper, to taste

crushed potato chips

## INSTRUCTIONS

Mix everything except chips. Sprinkle chips on top. Bake 25 minutes at 350°.

# Marinated Turkey Tenderloins

**Serves 6**

## INGREDIENTS

- **1** cup pineapple juice
- **¼** cup ketchup
- **2** tablespoons lemon juice
- **2** garlic cloves, minced
- **1** teaspoon prepared horseradish
- **½** teaspoon lemon pepper seasoning
- **¼** teaspoon curry powder
- **¼** teaspoon ground ginger
- **¼** teaspoon paprika
- **¼** teaspoon red pepper flakes
- **2** pounds turkey tenderloins

## INSTRUCTIONS

In a bowl, combine the first 10 ingredients. Mix well. Pour 1 cup into a large container. Add turkey. Refrigerate 8 hours or overnight for grilling. Drain and set aside marinade from turkey. Grill, covered, over medium to hot heat for 20–25 minutes, or until a meat thermometer reads 170°, turning every 6 minutes. Instead of grilling it, you can bake it in a roaster at 375° or 400° for 3 hours. Serve with remaining marinade as sauce.

# Turkey Casserole

**Serves 6**

## INGREDIENTS

- **12** slices bread
- **3** cups cooked turkey, cubed
- **1** cup celery, chopped
- **1** cup turkey broth
- **4** eggs, beaten
- **¼** cup butter, melted
- **1** (10¾-ounce) can cream of chicken soup
- **1** cup + **1** soup can's worth (10¾ ounces) milk, divided
- **2** cups cheese, grated
  salt and pepper, to taste
- **2** cups cracker crumbs, crushed

## INSTRUCTIONS

Place 12 slices of bread in 9 x 13-inch pan. Cover with cubed turkey and celery. Mix turkey broth, eggs, 1 cup milk, melted butter, salt, and pepper. Pour over turkey. Mix can of soup with 1 soup can's worth of milk. Place a layer of grated cheese over the turkey and pour the diluted soup over it. Top with cracker crumbs and bake, uncovered, at 350° for 35 minutes, or until bubbly. Serve with raw cabbage wedges.

# Duck-in-a-Nest

**Serves 6**

*We have a big pond on our farm and there are always plenty of ducks on it, and so that's usually what I serve when I invite the family to our place for dinner. I always make two plump ones and stuff them with bread filling. My sister told me that last Thanksgiving Day when they were on their way here, as soon as they could see our farm, their little four-year-old piped up, "Oh look, that's where the duck people live!"*

*Here are two recipes I changed over into duck dishes.*

## INGREDIENTS

*Nests*

**5–6** cups soft bread crumbs

**¼** cup onion, minced

**1** teaspoon celery salt

**⅛** teaspoon pepper

**½** cup butter or margarine, melted

**½** teaspoon poultry seasoning, optional

*Filling*

**⅓** cup butter or margarine

**⅓** cup flour

**½** cup light cream

**1½** cup milk

**½** teaspoon salt

**½** teaspoon pepper

**1** teaspoon Worcestershire sauce, optional

**3** cups cooked duck, chopped

**1** cup peas, optional

## INSTRUCTIONS

For nests, combine ingredients. Line 6 greased individual mini-casserole dishes with crumb mixture. Press into place and bake at 375° for 15 minutes, or until crumbs are brown.

To make the filling, melt butter and blend in flour. Add cream, milk, and seasonings. Cook until thickened, stirring constantly. Add duck and peas. Serve in crumb nests.

# Duck and Herb Stuffing

**Serves 6–8**

## INGREDIENTS

- **3** cups duck, chopped
- **½** cup duck broth
- **1** (10¾-ounce) can cream of celery soup
- **1** (10¾-ounce) can cream of mushroom soup
- **⅔** cup milk
- **½** cup margarine
- **1** (12-ounce) package herb stuffing or croutons

## INSTRUCTIONS

Stew duck and remove bones. Reserve ½ cup broth. Cube or chop duck and place in bottom of greased casserole dish. Mix soups with milk and pour over duck. Melt margarine and mix with broth. Mix this with stuffing. Place on top of soup and duck. Bake at 350° for 30 minutes.

**Variation:** Add 2 cups cooked macaroni and 1 cup grated cheese before baking.

# Cakes & Pies

# Black Midnight Cake

**Makes 1 (9 x 13-inch) cake**

*I often make this cake, since it is one of our favorites. One day I had just mixed all the dry ingredients when my busy toddler came in and wanted to help. I poured in the wet ingredients, ready to mix everything together. I turned my back and the toddler reached up to the counter and grabbed the bowl to peek in. He spilled most of the liquids down over himself and the floor. What a mess to clean up! I discovered that I had grabbed the bowl in time to save the dry ingredients. There was a bit of wetness there yet, so I just made a guess and added more wet ingredients again. I wasn't sure how it would turn out, but we wouldn't have known the difference.*

## INGREDIENTS

**2** cups flour
**1** cup brown sugar
**2** teaspoons baking powder
**¾** cup unsweetened cocoa powder
**1** teaspoon salt
**1** cup milk
**2** eggs
**1** teaspoon vanilla
**½** cup vegetable oil
**1** cup black coffee

## INSTRUCTIONS

Stir dry ingredients together. Add others in order as listed. Batter is very thin. Bake in a greased 9 x 13-inch pan at 350° for 35 minutes.

## Lucy's Kitchen Tip

Much less sugar can be used in cakes, cookies, and desserts without making them less tasty. Parents pay twice for sugar and sweets: when they buy them and when they pay the dentist.

# Moist Chocolate Cake

**Makes 1 (9 x 13-inch) cake**

*In 1993, when I was eleven years old, we lived in Pennsylvania. Mom and Dad went on a trip and left me in charge of the house and children. I had big plans for a beautifully clean house and perfect baked goods. So I got this simple recipe and baked this cake, which was a favorite to us all. But I had to make two, as one almost disappeared with a breakfast of warm oatmeal. You can imagine my proud feeling when Mom came home and saw this baked cake topped with a pudding-like frosting. In those years when eggs were scarce and we were still learning, we could easily make this cake without help.*

## INGREDIENTS

**3** cups flour

**2** cups sugar

**½** cup unsweetened cocoa powder

**2** teaspoons baking soda

**1** teaspoon salt

**2** teaspoons vinegar

**2** teaspoons vanilla

**2** cups water

**1** cup oil

## INSTRUCTIONS

Mix dry ingredients. Then add vinegar, vanilla, water, and oil. Mix well. Put in an ungreased 9 x 13-inch pan and bake at 350° for 30–40 minutes. Spread with Richmond Chocolate Frosting (p. 168) when cool.

# Ruth's Chocolate Cake

**Makes 2 (9 x 13-inch) cakes**

*I tell our children I almost grew up on Ruth's Chocolate Cake. Where or how it got the name, I don't know, but it was a family favorite, partly because it was easy to make, but mostly because it doesn't need eggs. We didn't have our own laying hens so we frequently ran out of eggs.*

*If I let my memory go back to the time we all gathered around the big table as children, I recall often eating partly thawed chocolate cake, soaked up in milk, with a generous helping of applesauce on top.*

## INGREDIENTS

**4** cups sugar

**½** cup unsweetened cocoa powder

**1** cup lard

**1½** cup hot water

**2** cups sour milk

**6** cups flour

**1** tablespoon baking soda

**1** tablespoon baking powder

**1** teaspoon vanilla

**1** teaspoon salt

## INSTRUCTIONS

In a big bowl, mix sugar, cocoa, and lard. Add hot water and milk. Add rest of ingredients, mixing well. Pour into 2 greased 9 x 13-inch pans. Bake at 350° for 30 minutes, until a toothpick inserted in middle comes out clean.

## Note:

May make 1 (11 x 15-inch) cake. Bake for 45 minutes.

# Cocoa Cupcakes

**Makes 24 cupcakes or 3 (8-inch) layers**

When I was about nine, I had the privilege of stirring up these cupcakes while Mom was sewing. All went well until I came to the stir-by-hand part. "Mom, does this really mean stir by hand?" I asked. "Yes," came the reply. Partway through the stirring process, I asked again, and another hurried yes was given. Suddenly the sewing machine quit its steady humming and I heard Mom's frantic voice, "Sarah, you didn't!" Each word came closer until she stood by my side. A sigh escaped her lips as she stared in disbelief at my hands sunken in the chocolate mess.

I always thought it was Sarah who learned a lesson that day, but since being a mother of little girls myself now, I wonder if Mom wasn't a little wiser as well!

## INGREDIENTS

- **1½** cup flour
- **1** teaspoon baking soda
- **1** cup granulated sugar
- **1** teaspoon salt
- **½** cup unsweetened cocoa powder
- **⅔** cup shortening
- **1** cup milk, divided
- **¾** teaspoon baking powder
- **2** eggs
- **1** teaspoon vanilla

## INSTRUCTIONS

Stir together flour, baking soda, sugar, salt, cocoa, shortening, and ⅔ cup milk vigorously by hand. Now stir in by itself baking powder. Add ⅓ cup milk, eggs, and vanilla. Blend by hand. Pour into medium-sized, lined cupcake tins (24 cupcakes total) or three greased 8-inch cake pans. Bake at 350° for about 15 minutes for cupcakes or about 25 minutes for cakes.

# Strawberry Long Cake

**Makes 1 (9 x 13-inch) cake**

*Strawberry season meant a lot of work for Mom and us two oldest girls, with ten younger siblings. We three would daily pick them by the ten-quart bucketful. Besides being a backbreaking task, we'd occasionally meet up with garter snakes. Eeek!*

*Mom's spirit was undaunted. She would rise early and pick a bucketful before we girls were up and had breakfast. Her example taught us to work, too.*

*I remember one time when I was in charge of babysitting, Grandpa passed by and saw Mom alone in the berry patch. He quoted, "Industrious mother—lazy girls. Lazy moms—industrious girls!" Thus I got an urge to prove to Grandpa that I'm not lazy!*

## INGREDIENTS

- **1** cup + **6** tablespoons sugar, divided
- **4** cups strawberries, sliced
- **2** cups + **3** tablespoons flour, divided
- **2** teaspoons baking powder
- **1** egg
- ½ teaspoon salt
- ⅓ cup shortening
- ⅔ cup milk
- ¼ cup butter, softened
- ¼ cup brown sugar

## INSTRUCTIONS

Sprinkle 1 cup sugar over strawberries. Let stand while preparing batter. Mix 2 cups flour, baking powder, 6 tablespoons sugar, egg, salt, shortening, and milk. Spread batter into a greased 9 x 13-inch cake pan and put berries over top of the batter. Cream together butter, brown sugar, and 3 tablespoons flour. Drop here and there over the strawberries. Bake at 350° until tester inserted in middle comes out clean, 20–30 minutes.

# Chocolate Filling

## INGREDIENTS

- **3** cups milk, divided
- **2** heaping tablespoons unsweetened cocoa powder
- **2** eggs
- ¾ cup flour
- **1** cup sugar
- **1** teaspoon vanilla

## INSTRUCTIONS

Bring 2½ cups milk to boil in saucepan. Mix remaining ½ cup milk with cocoa, eggs, and flour. Whisk into boiling milk along with sugar and stir until it boils again. Remove from heat. Add vanilla. Cool.

# Judith's Short Cake

**Makes 1 (9 x 13-inch) cake**

INGREDIENTS

**2** eggs

**½** cup water

**½** cup lard

**1** cup milk

**1½** teaspoon salt

**6** teaspoons baking powder

**4** tablespoons sugar

**4** cups flour

INSTRUCTIONS

Put everything in bowl and mix. Bake in 9 x 13-inch pan at 350° for 45 minutes, or until toothpick inserted in center comes out clean. Eat with berries and whipped cream.

# Rachel's Jelly Roll

**Serves 8–10**

*This jelly roll is an old recipe traced back to my mother, grandmother, and great-grandmother. It's so easy to make, and it just always gets nice. Other cake roll recipes don't turn out right for me. It's very good with icing, filling, or whatever you wish. One time when we had it for a family outing, my niece copied it for two different people. It's that good!*

INGREDIENTS

**2** eggs

**½** cup water

**½** cup lard

**1** cup milk

**1½** teaspoon salt

**6** teaspoons baking powder

**4** tablespoons sugar

**4** cups flour

INSTRUCTIONS

Put everything in bowl and mix. Bake in 9 x 13-inch pan at 350° for 45 minutes, or until toothpick inserted in center comes out clean. Eat with berries and whipped cream.

# Hawaiian Cake

**Makes 1 (9 x 9-inch) cake**

*One time I made this cake for company, and I felt it was a flop. I didn't know of anything I did wrong, but it seemed to stay so wet and heavy in the middle when it was supposed to be done baking. Finally, it looked too dark, so I took it out of the oven. A few hours later, I still wasn't pleased, so I quickly mixed another batch. Somehow this one satisfied me more. And I wasn't disappointed when my company the next day expressed how good the second cake was.*

*As it turned out, my husband couldn't find anything wrong with the first cake and he thinks I should make it more often anyway. So we had lots of yummy, moist cake to eat. You can hardly stop with one piece.*

## INGREDIENTS

- **2** cups white sugar
- **2** cups flour
- **1** teaspoon salt
- **2** teaspoons baking soda
- **1** cup English walnuts, chopped
- **1** teaspoon vanilla
- **2** eggs
- **1** (16-ounce) can crushed pineapple, undrained

*Topping*
- **1** (8-ounce) package cream cheese
- **½** cup margarine or butter
- **1⅓** cup confectioners' sugar
- **1** teaspoon vanilla
  nuts, chopped, and coconut, optional

## INSTRUCTIONS

Just pour everything together and mix. Very simple! Bake in greased 9 x 9-inch pan at 350° until golden brown, about 20 minutes. Allow to cool before mixing and spreading on topping. If desired, sprinkle with nuts and coconut. Yummy!

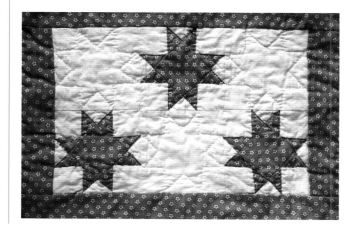

# Maplenut Chiffon Cake

**Makes 1 large tube cake**

*One year I made this Maplenut Chiffon cake for my mother's birthday. They live in the* Dawdy Haus *[house for grandparents] adjoining ours, and we had invited the other married children who live nearby to come over that evening.*

*This was supposed to be a surprise for them, and so I made the cake and covered it with plastic, being careful not to smudge the "Happy Birthday, Mommy" icing I had put on. While* Dawdy *and* Mommy *were napping, I smuggled the cake into their cellar so she wouldn't see it before we sang "Happy Birthday." We had also made custard for homemade vanilla ice cream, ready to be churned in the hand-crank ice cream freezer that evening.*

*When* Dawdy *got up from his nap, he went down to the cellar for something and saw the cake. He was keen enough not to tell Mommy, though, and we were able to surprise her. Our daughter slipped down to the cellar and put one candle on the cake for each decade of Mommy's life, lit them, and brought it upstairs. As soon as the cellar door opened, we all started to sing and Mommy had to wipe away tears.*

## INGREDIENTS

**2¼** cups flour

**¾** cup sugar

**1** tablespoon baking powder

**1** teaspoon salt

**¾** cup brown sugar

**½** cup vegetable oil

**5** egg yolks

**¾** cup cold water

**2** teaspoons maple extract

**1** cup egg whites, about 8 eggs

**½** teaspoon cream of tartar

**1** cup walnuts, chopped

## INSTRUCTIONS

Sift flour, sugar, baking powder, and salt into mixing bowl. Stir in brown sugar, vegetable oil, egg yolks, water, and maple extract. Beat until smooth. Combine egg whites and cream of tartar in mixing bowl. Beat until very stiff peaks form. Pour egg yolk batter in thin stream over egg whites. Gently fold in nuts. Pour into lightly greased tube pan. Bake at 325° for 55 minutes.

# Molasses Black Cake

**Makes 1 (9 x 13-inch) cake**

*Because this cake contains raisins, it was never a favorite of mine when I was young. I felt bad when Mom served it to our guest for breakfast. I held my breath as the cake was passed—hoping he wouldn't take a piece. My eyes dropped as he helped himself and I didn't glance up while he ate it. As the peaches and cake disappeared and the conversation continued, our guest kept glancing at the cake. Dad's idea about those glances differed greatly from mine, as he again handed the plate to our guest. I was rather surprised to hear our guest say, "This is the best cake I've ever tasted," as he reached for another piece.*

### INGREDIENTS

- **1** cup lard
- **1** cup brown sugar
- **1** egg
- **1** cup mild baking molasses
- **2⅔** cups flour
- **1** cup raisins
- **1** teaspoon baking soda
- **½** teaspoon cinnamon
- **½** teaspoon cloves
- **½** teaspoon nutmeg
- **1** cup strong coffee

### INSTRUCTIONS

Cream lard and brown sugar together until fluffy. Add egg and molasses and stir. Measure flour into a bowl. Take a tablespoon of the measured flour and mix with raisins in another bowl, and set aside. Add baking soda and spices to flour. Mix. Add flour mixture to lard mixture. Add coffee all at once; the batter will be thin. Fold in floured raisins. Pour into greased 9 x 13-inch pan. Bake at 350° for 55–60 minutes, until tester inserted in middle comes out clean.

# Applesauce Raisin Cake

**Makes 1 (9 x 13-inch) cake**

*When I was nine years old, my brother had his twelfth birthday, and I decided I wanted to make him a cake. Mom gave me permission to stir it together while he was busy in the barn doing the evening chores. I wanted to be so careful to do everything right, and thought I could do it without Mom's help. I made his favorite—applesauce cake—with raisins and chopped nuts stirred into the batter. I spread it carefully into the cake pan with a spatula and was proudly carrying it to the oven when Mom asked, "Are you sure you added baking soda?" I had forgotten! She helped me scoop it back into the bowl, and then I added the soda. The cake turned out surprisingly well, but not as nice as it would've been if I'd have added baking soda at the right time.*

## INGREDIENTS

- ½ cup butter, softened
- 1½ cup sugar
- 2 eggs
- 2½ cups flour
- ½ teaspoon salt
- 1 teaspoon cinnamon
- 1½ cup applesauce
- 1 teaspoon baking soda, dissolved in 2 tablespoons hot water
- ½ cup nuts, chopped
- 1 cup raisins

## INSTRUCTIONS

Cream butter and sugar. Add eggs. Mix dry ingredients and add alternately with applesauce. Add baking soda/water, nuts, and raisins. Bake in a greased 9 x 13-inch pan at 350° for approximately 35 minutes.

# Cherry Coffee Cake

## Makes 1 (9 x 13-inch) cake

*This is one of our favorite "cakes" to make when we want something special. It is so special in looks and flavor and yet needs only ordinary ingredients. We make it with or without glaze. We also make different flavors. So far we have tried apricot and plum besides sour cherries. Red or purplish plums give the filling a deep ruby red color that, with the white drizzled frosting, looks like something out of the store.*

*We use a quart jar of our own canned fruit that was thickened before canning. Sometimes we use fresh fruit and thicken it just before baking.*

*We have made these bars for family gatherings, picnics, and hot lunches for school, and it seems everyone likes them.*

### INGREDIENTS

**1** cup butter, softened

**1¼** cup sugar

**4** eggs

**1** teaspoon vanilla

**3** cups flour

**1½** teaspoon baking powder

**½** teaspoon salt

**1** (21-ounce) can cherry pie filling

*Glaze*

**1** cup confectioners' sugar

**1** tablespoon butter, melted

**2** tablespoons milk

### INSTRUCTIONS

Cream butter and sugar. Add eggs one at a time and beat well. Add vanilla. Blend in remaining ingredients except pie filling. Place two-thirds of batter in greased 9 x 13-inch baking pan. Spread pie filling over batter. Drop remaining batter by teaspoonfuls over top of cherries. Bake at 350° for 30–40 minutes. Cool. Make glaze: Combine confectioners' sugar and melted butter. Stir in milk to reach spreading consistency.

# White Mountain Cake

**Makes 1 (9 x 13-inch) cake**

*This is a cake my husband's aunt baked. We like to go to visit them about once a year. One time a group of us went to visit them with two horses hitched to a double buggy. We stopped at a nice pond to fish. We discovered we could catch big bass with little blue gills for bait. So while we women cleaned the fish, the men took some little blue gills and tried to catch big bass. We got to the aunt's house that evening and fried some fish for our supper.*

*The next day, my husband kept smelling something; it kept getting worse, but if he went outside, he didn't smell it as much so he thought, well, that's just the way my aunt's house smells. In the evening before we started home, he got a paper out of his pliers pocket and it was wet and smelly. Here was a stinky little blue gill he forgot to take out of his pocket!*

## INGREDIENTS

**1¾** cup sugar

**1** cup cream

**1** cup milk

**1** teaspoon vanilla

**3** cups flour

**1** tablespoon baking powder

**½** teaspoon salt

**½** cup oil

**2** eggs, separated

*Topping*

**¾** cup brown sugar

**1** cup grated coconut

**¼** cup cream

**½** cup butter, melted

**1** teaspoon vanilla

## INSTRUCTIONS

Mix everything together except egg whites. Beat the 2 egg whites until stiff peaks form. Fold in. Pour into greased 9 x 13-inch pan. Bake cake for 40 minutes at 350°. Meanwhile, boil topping ingredients 1 minute and spread over hot cake. Return cake to the oven and bake 5 more minutes.

# Katie's Yellow Cake

**Makes 1 (9-inch) cake**

*I was ten years old when I baked this cake for my mother's birthday when my parents were gone for the afternoon. I had helped with baking before but had never done it alone. My fifteen-year-old brother stoked up the fire for me. When the oven was hot, I put in my cake and sat down to wait. It turned out beautifully! Because I wanted to have all evidence cleared away by the time my parents returned, I frosted it soon after taking it from the oven. Then it was safely hidden away.*

*When we celebrated Mother's birthday, the cake was rather soggy because some of the frosting had soaked in. Mother knew right away that I must have frosted it while warm! To this day, I often think of that when I frost a cake.*

## INGREDIENTS

- **1** cup white sugar
- **2** eggs
- **1** teaspoon vanilla
- **1** cup sweet cream
- **2** teaspoons baking powder
- **1½** cup flour

## INSTRUCTIONS

Stir together. Pour into greased 9-inch cake pan and bake at 350° for 30 minutes.

# Richmond Chocolate Frosting

**Makes enough for 1 (9 x 13-inch) cake**

## INGREDIENTS

- **1** cup sugar
- **3** tablespoons cornstarch
- **⅓** cup unsweetened cocoa powder
  dash salt
- **1** cup boiling water
- **1** teaspoon vanilla
- **3** tablespoons butter

## INSTRUCTIONS

Mix dry ingredients in saucepan. Add boiling water and cook, stirring, until thick. Remove from heat. Add butter and vanilla and stir.

# Cream Cheese Frosting

**Makes 2 cups**

*I'm a nine-year-old Amish girl who likes to help her mom bake and ice cakes. Licking the bowl is the fun part! This icing is very good on most any cake.*

### INGREDIENTS

**1** tablespoon milk

**1** teaspoon vanilla

**3** ounces (⅓ cup) cream cheese, softened

**6** tablespoons butter, softened

**1¾** cup confectioners' sugar

### INSTRUCTIONS

Mix milk, vanilla, cream cheese, and butter. Add sugar and beat until smooth.

# Fluffy White Frosting

**Frosts 2 (8- or 9-inch) layers or 1 (9 x 13-inch) cake**

*This frosting is a favorite of mine because it's so simple to make and turns out right for me. When we make a special cake at our house, it usually gets this frosting.*

*We have often used it on a sponge cake and put a variety of toppings or decorations on top. I sometimes color the frosting, too. Once we had tiny tangerines, which we peeled, putting one tiny slice on each piece of cake. Another time we put heartnut pieces on each slice. One time it was chocolate cake, I believe, and we flavored the frosting with peppermint and sprinkled green sugar crystals all over.*

### INGREDIENTS

**¾** cup sugar

**¼** cup light corn syrup

**2** tablespoons water

**2** egg whites

**¼** teaspoon cream of tartar

**¼** teaspoon salt

**1** teaspoon vanilla extract

### INSTRUCTIONS

In top of double boiler, combine sugar, corn syrup, water, egg whites, cream of tartar, and salt. Cook over rapidly boiling water, beating with mixer or rotary beater until mixture stands in peaks. Remove from heat; add vanilla extract. Continue beating until frosting holds deep swirls.

# Best-Ever Shoofly Pie

**Makes 8 (9-inch) pies**

*I was baking bread and icing buns for a produce stand when someone informed me that a man was asking for shoofly pies and they were sending him over. Oh my! Pies are my thing, but for sure not shoofly pies!*

*I tried some recipes and the guy said they weren't moist enough. I tried more recipes, and he just wasn't satisfied with them. So I started asking people who were in the business of baking shoofly pies for market. I got a market recipe and tried it, but they cooked over so bad that I had a smoky kitchen and had to wash off the walls. I was getting discouraged, but I decided to try the recipe again and fill eight pie crusts with it instead of only six. They turned out fine, and the guy said that's the way he likes them.*

*I got more customers and many favorable comments. At one time I baked a hundred a day, and shared my recipe with others who wanted to bake shoofly pies for market.*

## INGREDIENTS

- **8** cups pastry flour
- **4½** cups brown sugar
- **7** tablespoons lard
- **6** eggs
- **6** cups molasses or table syrup
- **6** cups boiling water, divided
- **6** teaspoons baking soda
- **8** (9-inch) pie crusts, unbaked

## INSTRUCTIONS

Mix dry ingredients and lard into nice, even fine crumbs. Take out 2 cups crumbs and set aside. In a big mixing bowl, beat the eggs and add the molasses. Then add 4½ cups boiling water and mix well. Dissolve baking soda in 1½ cup boiling water and add it to the molasses mixture. Add the crumbs and stir until smooth. Pour into unbaked pie crusts and sprinkle the 2 cups reserved crumbs evenly on top. Bake at 400° for 10 minutes, or until they start to puff up a little, then turn oven back to 350° and bake another 30 minutes until done.

# Amish Vanilla Pie

**Makes 1 (9-inch) pie**

### INGREDIENTS

*Part one*

½ cup brown sugar

**1** tablespoon flour

¼ cup corn syrup

**1** cup water

**1** egg, beaten

**1** teaspoon vanilla

*Part two*

½ cup brown sugar

¼ cup butter

**1** cup flour

⅛ teaspoon salt

½ teaspoon baking soda

½ teaspoon cream of tartar

### INSTRUCTIONS

Part one: Combine in 2-quart saucepan. Cook over medium heat, stirring until it comes to a boil. Let cool.

Part two: Mix in a bowl until crumbly.

Pour cooled part-one mixture into an unbaked 9-inch pie crust. Top with crumbs from part two. Bake at 350° for 40 minutes, or until golden brown.

# Peanut Butter Fudge Pie

**Makes 1 (9-inch) pie**

*A rich, extravagant pie that is great for special occasions or to impress special people.*

### INGREDIENTS

**1** cup creamy peanut butter

**1** (8-ounce) package cream cheese, softened

½ cup sugar

**12** ounces whipped topping, divided

**1** (9-inch) graham cracker crust

**1** cup fudge topping

### INSTRUCTIONS

Beat together peanut butter, cream cheese, and sugar. Gently fold in 3 cups whipped topping. Spoon into pie crust. Soften fudge topping in microwave for 1 minute. Cool slightly, then spoon over the pie filling. Refrigerate until serving time, then spread the remaining whipped topping over the fudge layer. Garnish with more fudge topping, if desired. May be served partially frozen, if desired.

## Caramel Pecan Pie

**Makes 1 (9-inch) pie**

### INGREDIENTS

- **3** eggs, well beaten
- **1** cup brown sugar
- **¾** cup light Karo syrup
- **1** tablespoon butter, melted
  pinch salt
- **1** cup pecan halves
- **1** (9-inch) pie crust, unbaked

### INSTRUCTIONS

Mix and pour into pie crust. Bake at 325° for 50 minutes, or until set. Serve with whipped cream.

## Union Pie

**Makes 3 (9-inch) pies**

### INGREDIENTS

- **2** cups sugar
- **2** cups sour cream
- **4** tablespoons flour
- **1** teaspoon baking soda
- **2** cups baking molasses
- **2** cups buttermilk
- **4** eggs, beaten
- **1** teaspoon lemon flavoring
- **3** (9–inch) pie crusts, unbaked

### INSTRUCTIONS

Mix and pour into unbaked pie crusts. Bake at 350° until toothpick comes clean in center, about 45–50 minutes.

# Mama's Mince Pie

**Makes 2 (9-inch) pies**

*When butchering was over every winter, my mother would make a crock of mincemeat for pies. She would put bits of beef and pork in the old iron kettle on the big cooking range in the kitchen, then add the rest of the ingredients.*

*I can remember her standing in front of the stove, wearing her long gingham apron with her wooden spoon stirring and stirring, sometimes humming old-fashioned tunes. For the mincemeat she'd stir in chopped apples, raisins, brown sugar, spices, homemade dandelion wine, and probably more things I can't remember.*

*Since we don't do our own butchering anymore, I hardly ever make mince pie anymore. But we do buy one every now and then, just to savor the unique taste that brings old-time memories floating back!*

## INGREDIENTS

- **1** cup ground beef
- **1** cup pork, shredded
- **6** cups apples, chopped
- **1** cup raisins
- **3** tablespoons dandelion wine or vinegar
- **1** tablespoon butter, melted
- **2** cups brown sugar
- **1** teaspoon cinnamon
- **1** teaspoon allspice
-     salt, to taste
- **2** (9-inch) pie crusts, unbaked

## INSTRUCTIONS

Mix all together, then pour into unbaked pie crusts. Bake at 350° for 35 minutes.

## Susan's Coconut Pie

**Makes 1 (8-inch) pie**

*This was my mother's favorite recipe and is still a favorite of ours to this day. My mother died about three years ago, but her recipe lives on. I have a family of ten, and each one likes it. It is smooth and creamy if you bake it with a slow oven and do not let it boil. Use your choice of coconut, sweetened or unsweetened, fine or coarse—all options are fine.*

### INGREDIENTS

- ½ cup sugar (scant)
- 1 small egg yolk
- ½ cup cream
- ½ cup milk
- 1 tablespoon flour
- ½ cup shredded coconut
- 2 egg whites
- 1 (8-inch) pie crust, unbaked

### INSTRUCTIONS

Mix everything together except the egg whites. Beat the egg whites until stiff peaks form, and fold into the filling. Pour into pie crust. Bake at 325° until set, 35–45 minutes.

### Note

I like to prebake the pie crust for 15 minutes before adding the filling

## Lemon Meringue Pie

**Makes 1 (9-inch) pie**

### INGREDIENTS

- 1⅓ cup sugar, divided
- ¼ cup cornstarch
- 1½ cup cold water
- 3 egg yolks, slightly beaten
- ¼ cup lemon juice
- 1 tablespoon butter
- 1 (9-inch) pie crust, baked
- 3 egg whites

### INSTRUCTIONS

In medium saucepan, combine 1 cup sugar and cornstarch. Gradually stir in water until smooth. Stir in beaten egg yolks. Stirring constantly, bring to boil over medium heat and boil 1 minute. Remove from heat. Stir in lemon juice and butter. Spoon hot filling into pie crust. In small bowl, beat egg whites until foamy. Gradually beat in ⅓ cup sugar, beating until stiff peaks form. Spread over pie, sealing the edges. Bake 15–20 minutes at 350°, or until golden brown.

# Pineapple Coconut Pie

**Makes 1 (9-inch) pie**

*One time I helped a neighbor who had a new baby by doing a bit of baking. The lady told me to make pies, whatever I wanted. Not knowing the family's likes or dislikes, I was a bit undecided.*

*When suppertime came, they asked, "What kind did you make?" I said, "Pineapple coconut." They never heard of it before but liked it very much, and the pies didn't last long. I also had a brother at home who didn't like pineapple, but we could always make this kind without telling him and he'd eat it. Now I have a husband who also dislikes pineapple but loves coconut. So one of these days I'll surprise him yet.*

### INGREDIENTS

**3** eggs

**1** cup sugar

**1** tablespoon cornstarch

**½** cup drained crushed pineapple

**½** cup corn syrup

**¼** cup shredded coconut

**¼** cup margarine or butter, melted

**1** (9-inch) pie crust, unbaked

### INSTRUCTIONS

Mix all together. Pour into pie crust and bake at 350° for 45–50 minutes.

# Rhubarb Pie

**Makes 1 (9-inch) pie**

*I used this recipe the first time I baked rhubarb pie when I was eleven years old. It was in the spring, and most of our family had gone out of state for a wedding. They left me and three of my brothers at home to do chores. I felt very responsible to do the cooking, but being next to the youngest in a family of ten children, I didn't have much experience.*

*I decided to bake a pie. I had no idea how many crusts one recipe would make. I ended up with six pie crusts, so I made six pies. I had quite a time to get the crusts rolled and fitted in the pans.*

*Well, I was in the midst of my baking mess and here comes the egg delivery man, who delivered ten dozen eggs to us every week. He knew most of the family was not home, so he asked what I intended to do with so many pies. "Well," I replied, "I thought it would be nice to have pie on hand when the rest of the family returned home." But lo and behold, the pies were all gone by the time the others came home!*

*The next week when he came with eggs, he complimented Mother to have raised a daughter like me. By now, my face was red and I slipped into another room. Mother told him the pies were all eaten before they got home, but that I did a good job in supplying food for the table, including pies, even though it wasn't the softest crust.*

*But I must say rolling the crust went better after that experience. And I still like rhubarb pie.*

## INGREDIENTS

**1½** cup rhubarb, chopped

**1** cup milk

**1¼** cup sugar

butter the size of a walnut, softened

**1** egg, beaten

**2½** tablespoons flour

**1** (9-inch) pie crust, unbaked

## INSTRUCTIONS

Mix well and pour into an unbaked pie crust. Bake at 350° for 30 minutes.

## Lucy's Kitchen Tip

When making custard pies, warm the milk before mixing with the eggs and the rest of the ingredients. This shortens the baking time and helps to keep the pie crust crisp.

# Blueberry Pie

**Makes 1 (9-inch) pie**

*A few years ago we had a yard sale, and I made a dozen of these blueberry pies to sell along with homemade bread and bars. Every one of the pies was sold within a half hour of opening time, and I found myself taking orders for more.*

*One woman happened to drop her pie on the way out to her car, and she was so disappointed that she cried. She said it was her husband's birthday and his favorite kind of pie. An elderly gentleman heard her talking about it, and gave her the pie he had bought! This brought more tears to her eyes. How thankful we are that there are still some very kind and generous people in this world.*

## INGREDIENTS

- **2½** cups fresh blueberries
- **1** cup sugar, plus more for sprinkling
- **2** tablespoons flour
- **2** tablespoons minute tapioca
- **⅛** teaspoon salt
- **1** double-crust pastry for 9-inch pie
- **1** tablespoon lemon juice
- **2** tablespoons butter

## INSTRUCTIONS

Toss blueberries with sugar, flour, tapioca, and salt. Pour into pastry shell. Dribble lemon juice over blueberry mixture and dot with butter. Wet pastry edge with fingertips and cover with top pastry. Cut several vents. Sprinkle with sugar. Bake at 350° for 45 minutes, or until done.

# Glazed Peach Pie

**Makes 1 (9-inch) pie**

*After my sister-in-law shared this recipe, I was amazed how good it is for the small amount of ingredients it requires. Peeling peaches takes me back in memory to when I was a little girl. We enjoyed watching Mom peel a whole peach without breaking the "chain" it created. She told us of how her mother always made "peach peeling" pie.*

*"Yuck!" was our comment—until Mom reminded us how we liked to sneak some of the peelings out of the bowl when she wasn't looking.*

### INGREDIENTS

**7** large peaches

**1** cup sugar

**2½** teaspoons cornstarch

**1** 9-inch pie crust, baked
whipped cream

### INSTRUCTIONS

Mash 3 peaches, or enough to make 1 cup. Combine mashed peaches, sugar, and cornstarch in saucepan, cooking and stirring until thick. Cool. Put small amount of cooled glaze in bottom of baked pie shell. Slice remaining 4 peaches on top and cover with remaining glaze. Top with whipped cream.

# Peach Cream Pie

**Makes 1 (9-inch) pie**

## INGREDIENTS

*Crust*

½  cup butter

1½ cup flour

½  teaspoon salt

*Filling*

4  cups fresh peaches, sliced

1  cup sugar, divided

2  tablespoons flour

¼  teaspoon salt

½  teaspoon vanilla

1  cup sour cream

1  egg

*Topping*

⅓  cup sugar

½  cup butter

⅓  cup flour

1  teaspoon cinnamon

## INSTRUCTIONS

Make crust: Cut butter into flour and salt. Press dough into 9-inch pie pan. Make filling: In a mixing bowl, sprinkle peaches with ¼ cup sugar. Let stand while preparing rest of filling. Combine ¾ cup sugar, flour, egg, salt, and vanilla. Fold in sour cream. Stir in peaches and pour into crust. Combine topping ingredients and sprinkle over top. Bake at 400° for 45–55 minutes.

# Strawberry Pie

**Makes 3 (9-inch) pies**

## INGREDIENTS

6  cups crushed berries

2½ cups sugar

12 tablespoons instant Clear Jel

3  (9-inch) pie crusts, baked

## INSTRUCTIONS

Mix the instant Clear Jel with the sugar. Slowly sprinkle the mixture over the crushed berries and beat constantly until thick. Divide equally among three baked pie crusts.

*Note*

Can use this recipe with peaches, too.

# Dutch Apple Pie

**Makes 1 (9-inch) pie**

*I still think back fondly to my mother's pie-making days when I wasn't old enough to go to school yet. She always gave me a little ball of dough and let me use the rolling pin to roll it out to fit a little four-inch pie tin. She usually made either cherry, apple, peach, or raisin pies, and gave me some of the filling for my little pie. Then she showed me how to make a design on the piece I had rolled out for the top crust with the tip of the knife. After it was on, we fluted the edge, then poked holes in the crust to let out the steam. Sometimes we stuck dry macaroni into the holes so they wouldn't close up.*

*Mother always made me feel like I was such a big help to her, which makes me smile now. Pie doesn't taste as good to me anymore as it did then. Maybe it was the love she put in!*

### INGREDIENTS

- **1** cup brown sugar
- **3** tablespoons flour
- **1** teaspoon cinnamon
- **4** tablespoons butter
- **3** cups apples, sliced
- **3** tablespoons cream
- **1** (9-inch) pie crust, unbaked

### INSTRUCTIONS

Combine flour, sugar, and cinnamon. Cut in butter with a pastry blender. Place sliced apples in pie crust. Sprinkle crumb mixture over top. Drizzle with cream. Bake at 375° for 35 minutes, or until apples are soft and a rich syrup has formed.

# Delicious Pumpkin Pie

**Makes 1 (9-inch) pie**

*This recipe was used at a wedding. Dad liked it so well he asked Mother to get the recipe. It is now our family's favorite. When I ask what kind of pie they want, they all say, "Delicious Pumpkin!" It seems we never have enough pumpkins in the garden.*

### INGREDIENTS

**1** cup brown sugar

**2** tablespoons flour

**1** teaspoon cinnamon

**¼** teaspoon salt

**2** tablespoons margarine

**1** teaspoon vanilla

**1** (15-ounce) can pumpkin or butternut squash

**2** egg yolks

**1½** cup milk

**2** egg whites, stiffly beaten

**1** (9-inch) deep-dish pie crust, unbaked

### INSTRUCTIONS

Mix ingredients together well, folding in beaten egg whites by hand at the end. Pour into pie crust. Bake at 350° for 40–50 minutes, until set in the middle. Chill well before serving.

# Aunt Elsie's Pumpkin Pie

## Makes 2 (9-inch) pies

*For years, I always looked forward to Aunt Elsie's pumpkin pie at family gatherings. It was the accepted thing: Aunt Elsie would bring pumpkin pie.*

*Aunt Elsie once told me that the honey really puts a touch to it. And, yes, it sure does! I could eat half a pie all by myself! I can almost never stop with just one piece.*

*Recently, her daughters were looking through their mother's recipes and I happened to be near and spotted this one. I was so pleased to get a copy of it so now I, too, can make it.*

### INGREDIENTS

**1¼** cup cooked pumpkin or, preferably, butternut squash

**½** cup sugar

**⅓** cup honey

**2** eggs, beaten

**1** cup milk

**2** tablespoons water

**½** teaspoon vanilla

**¼** teaspoon cloves

**1** teaspoon cinnamon

**½** teaspoon salt

**1** teaspoon flour

**2** (9-inch) pie crusts, unbaked

### INSTRUCTIONS

Mix pie filling ingredients and pour into pie crusts. Bake at 400° for 45–60 minutes, until set.

# Grape Tarts

**Makes 6 tarts**

## INGREDIENTS

½ cup grape juice

**1** cup sugar

½ cup water

**5** teaspoons cornstarch

**1** cup grapes, halved and seeded

**6** tart shells

whipped cream

**6** nice grapes, for garnish

## INSTRUCTIONS

Bring grape juice, sugar, and water to boiling point. Blend cornstarch to a smooth paste with a little cold water and stir in. Add grapes to the mixture and simmer until the grapes are soft and mixture is thick. Turn into tart shells. Chill. Top with whipped cream and 1 raw grape on each tart.

# Half-Moon Pies

**Serves 12–15**

## INGREDIENTS

**1** quart dried apple slices (known as *schnitz*)

1½ cup water

**1** quart applesauce

1½ cup brown sugar

½ teaspoon cinnamon

## INSTRUCTIONS

Boil the dried apple slices in the water until soft and no water remains. Drain through a colander and add the rest of the ingredients.

Make pie crust (Never-Fail Pie Crust recipe on p. 186 works well) and divide into balls the size of a large egg. Roll out each piece as thin as pie crust. Fold over to make a crease through the center. Unfold again and make 2 holes in top part of dough. On the other half, place ½ cup of the filling. Wet the edge and fold over to make a half moon. Press edges together. Cut off the remaining dough with a pie crimper. Brush top with buttermilk or beaten egg. Bake at 450° until brown, about 15 minutes.

# Oatmeal Pie Crust

**Makes 1 (9-inch) pie crust**

*This crust can be used for your favorite pie filling but is especially good with apples. Bake several crusts and freeze them for a handy meal during busy seasons. Young girls can handle these crusts better than those that require a rolling pin.*

### INGREDIENTS

¾ cup melted butter

½ cup brown sugar

½ teaspoon salt

½ teaspoon baking soda

1¾ cup flour

1½ cup quick oats

### INSTRUCTIONS

Mix together and press into a 9-inch pie plate. Bake at 350° until golden brown, about 10–15 minutes. Delicious filled with cooked apple pie filling.

# Never-Fail Pie Crust

**Makes enough pastry for 4 pies**

### INGREDIENTS

4 cups flour

1 cup shortening

1 cup water

### INSTRUCTIONS

Cut flour and shortening into crumbs. Add 1 cup water and mix gently to form dough. Divide into four balls, roll out each with rolling pin, and gently transfer to pie plates.

## Lucy's Kitchen Tip

Use milk in pie crusts instead of water for a browner crust. Milk can also be brushed over the top before baking.

# My Best Pie Pastry

**Makes pastry for 3 double (9-inch) crusts**

*I worked out as a hired girl for different people, and they often gave me the job of doing the weekly baking because they knew I liked it. It was when I was working for a family in Bedford County, Pennsylvania, that the Mrs. suggested I could bake pies. I told her about my poor pie-baking record. My crusts turned out so hard that my brothers suggested using a butcher knife to cut them. My dad, who had digestive problems and hardly any teeth, couldn't even eat my pies.*

*But she said, "Oh, I have an excellent recipe that makes such nice crusts." I didn't have much faith in it, but I tried. To my surprise, they turned out good!*

*So I copied the recipe in my homemade cookbook to take along home. I used it to make pies for my dad, and when he tasted them, he said, "Oh, if you bake crusts like these, I can eat pie, too." I never tried any other recipe since!*

## INGREDIENTS

**5** cups flour

**½** teaspoon salt

**½** teaspoon baking powder

**1½** cup lard

**2** egg yolks

cold water

## INSTRUCTIONS

Combine dry ingredients and work in the lard. Place egg yolks in a 1-cup measure, stir with a fork until smooth. Add cold water to make 1 scant cupful. Stir again. Sprinkle gradually over the dry ingredients, toss with a fork to make a soft dough (I use my hands). Roll out for pie crust as usual.

Cookies

# Clara's Sugar Cookies

**Makes about 10 dozen**

*This is the recipe my mother used when she baked cookies. She never ceased to get compliments on these. She would often make a double batch to feed her family of ten children. I can remember eating as many as six cookies at a time if Mother didn't notice. She always wanted us to eat the ones that were a little burnt first.*

*Now I also use this recipe, especially when I am baking for church. And my little girl seems to like these as well as I did. I have heard the compliment, "You have your mother's talent for baking cookies."*

## INGREDIENTS

**6** eggs

**8** teaspoons baking soda

**1** cup hot water

**2** cups white sugar

**4** cups brown sugar

**2** cups lard

**2** cups sour milk

**2** cups sour cream

**4** teaspoons vanilla

**10** teaspoons baking powder

**2** teaspoons salt

**4** tablespoons lemon extract

**12** cups flour

## INSTRUCTIONS

Beat eggs. Dissolve baking soda in water. Add to eggs. Add rest of ingredients, stirring to make a stiff dough. Now drop onto cookie sheets and flatten a little. Bake in 400° or 425° oven for 8–10 minutes.

# Soft Sugar Cookies

**Makes about 6 dozen**

*My baked goods were getting low and it was getting hard to pack my husband's lunch. So I fixed some Jell-O, baked bread, and stirred up these cookies, a new recipe for me. I decided to make some horse-shaped ones for the little boy next door for his lunch. I filled a container of heart-shaped ones for a young family who have two little boys whose father cannot always be at home. So when you make these cookies, don't forget to share. Bake someone happy!*

## INGREDIENTS

**2** cups margarine

**3** cups sugar

**4** eggs

**2** cups cream or evaporated milk

**2** teaspoons baking soda

**6** teaspoons baking powder

**½** teaspoon salt

**1** teaspoon lemon extract

**5** cups flour (approximately— enough to make a stiff dough)

## INSTRUCTIONS

Cream together margarine and sugar. Add eggs and stir well. Add rest of ingredients. Chill overnight. Roll out on lightly floured board, cut into shapes, and bake at 350° for 8–10 minutes.

# Pumpkin Cookies

**Makes 2 dozen**

*My friend gave me this recipe. I always make about six batches. We have a family of nine so it always takes a lot of cookies. I like these because they are so moist and don't need frosting, and still they are everyone's favorite.*

## INGREDIENTS

- **1** cup cooked pumpkin, mashed
- **1** cup sugar
- **½** cup oil
- **1** egg
- **1** teaspoon vanilla
- **1** teaspoon baking soda
- **1** tablespoon milk
- **2** teaspoons baking powder
- **1** teaspoon cinnamon
- **½** teaspoon salt
- **2** cups flour
- **1** cup chocolate chips
- **½** cup nuts

## INSTRUCTIONS

Mix pumpkin, sugar, oil, egg, and vanilla and beat until smooth. Dissolve baking soda in milk. Add to bowl. Add baking powder, cinnamon, and salt. Add flour. Last of all, add chocolate chips and nuts. Drop onto baking sheets. Bake at 375° for about 10 minutes.

# Chocolate Chip Cookies

**Makes about 4 dozen**

*These chocolate chip cookies are my favorite. Once when I went to my friend's yard sale, there were some there for sale, so I bought some and they were just so good and white. I decided it must be because the recipe used all white sugar. So I asked my friend for the recipe and to my surprise, it contained only brown sugar.*

*We used to have cookie day in school. Once a year, every family brought cookies along. Then we set them on the table and we could eat all we wanted of any kind all day, except at recess time. These cookies are perfect for that!*

### INGREDIENTS

- **2** cups butter or oil
- **3** cups brown sugar
- **4** eggs
- **2** teaspoons vanilla
- **2** teaspoons baking soda
- **2** teaspoons salt
- **5** cups flour
- **1** cup chocolate chips

### INSTRUCTIONS

Mix all ingredients in order given. Drop onto ungreased baking sheets by spoonful. Bake at 350° for 8–10 minutes.

# M&M Jumbo Cookies

**Makes about 5 dozen big cookies**

### INGREDIENTS

- **2** cups shortening, soft
- **3** cups sugar
- **4** eggs
- **4** tablespoons milk
- **1** teaspoon vanilla
- **7** cups flour
- **1** tablespoon baking soda
- **1** tablespoon baking powder
- **1** teaspoon salt
- **2** cups M&M's
- **1** cup nuts or raisins, optional

### INSTRUCTIONS

Mix shortening, sugar, and eggs. Stir in milk and vanilla. Separately, stir together rest of ingredients. Add to egg mixture and stir. Roll into balls the size of a walnut and place about 3 inches apart on ungreased cookie sheet. Flatten with fork dipped in flour, making a crisscross pattern. Bake at 350° for 10 minutes.

# Aunt Fannie's Chocolate Chip Cookies

**Makes about 4 dozen**

*Cookies—what a favorite for our family! We have four girls and two boys, so a batch of cookies never lasts long. In fact, most times I double this recipe. They also like plenty of milk to drink with cookies, and since we have a dairy farm of sixty cows, there is plenty of good fresh milk around.*

*I got this recipe from my Aunt Fannie, and since I started using it, I don't use any other chocolate chip recipe. Hope you will enjoy it, too.*

### INGREDIENTS

**1½** cup vegetable oil

**1½** cup brown sugar

**1½** cup white sugar

**4** eggs, beaten

**2** teaspoons vanilla

**2** teaspoons water

**2** teaspoons baking soda

**1** teaspoon salt

**4½** cups flour

**1½** cup chocolate chips

### INSTRUCTIONS

Mix oil, sugars, and eggs. Add vanilla, water, baking soda, and salt. Add chocolate chips and flour. Drop by teaspoon onto greased cookie sheets. Bake at 350° for 10 minutes, or until light brown.

# Gumdrop Cookies

**Makes about 10 dozen**

### INGREDIENTS

**2** cups sugar

**2** cups confectioners' sugar

**4** eggs

**2** teaspoons salt

**9** cups flour

**2** teaspoons baking soda

**2** teaspoons cream of tartar

**2** teaspoons vanilla

**1½** cup nuts, chopped

**2** cups gumdrops

### INSTRUCTIONS

Mix in order given. Chill dough. Roll into 1½-inch balls and flatten on baking sheet. Bake at 350° for 10–12 minutes.

# Amish Hats
# (Chocolate Marshmallow Cookies)

**Makes 3 dozen**

## INGREDIENTS

**1¾** cup flour

**½** teaspoon salt

**½** cup unsweetened cocoa powder

**½** teaspoon baking soda

**½** cup shortening

**1** cup brown sugar

**1** egg

**1** teaspoon vanilla

**¼** cup milk

**18** large marshmallows, halved

*Cocoa Frosting*

**2** cups confectioners' sugar

**5** teaspoons unsweetened cocoa powder

**5** teaspoons cream

**1** tablespoon butter

pinch salt

## INSTRUCTIONS

Sift together flour, salt, cocoa, and baking soda. Cream shortening and brown sugar. Add egg, vanilla, and milk, beating well. Add dry ingredients and mix by hand. Drop by teaspoonful onto baking sheets. Bake 10 minutes at 350°. Remove from oven and press half a marshmallow, cut-side down, on each cookie. Bake 1 minute longer. Cool and top with frosting. Make frosting: Combine ingredients in small bowl and stir until creamy.

# Mocha-Frosted Dreams

**Makes 4 dozen**

## INGREDIENTS

- **½** cup shortening
- **1** square (1 ounce) unsweetened chocolate
- **1** cup brown sugar
- **1** egg
- **1** teaspoon vanilla
- **½** cup sour milk
- **1½** cup flour
- **½** teaspoon baking powder
- **½** teaspoon baking soda
- **¼** teaspoon salt
- **½** cup nuts, chopped
- **1** cup chocolate chips

*Frosting*

- **¼** cup butter
- **2** tablespoons unsweetened cocoa powder
- **2** teaspoons instant coffee
  pinch salt
- **2½** cups confectioners' sugar
- **1** teaspoon vanilla
- **2** tablespoons milk (approximately)

## INSTRUCTIONS

Melt shortening and chocolate in pan. Stir in brown sugar. Remove from heat. Beat in egg, vanilla, and sour milk. Sift together dry ingredients and add to chocolate mixture. Stir in nuts and chips. Drop by heaping teaspoonful onto greased cookie sheet. Bake at 375° for 10 minutes. Make frosting: Cream butter, cocoa, coffee, and salt. Beat in sugar, vanilla, and enough milk, teaspoon by teaspoon, for spreading consistency. Frost cookies when cool.

# Soft Oatmeal Cookies

**Makes 5 dozen**

## INGREDIENTS

- **1** cup oil
- **2** eggs
- **1¼** cup sugar
- **⅓** cup baking molasses
- **1¾** cup flour
- **1** teaspoon salt
- **1** teaspoon baking soda
- **1** teaspoon cinnamon
- **2** cups quick oats
- **1** cup raisins
- **½** cup nuts

## INSTRUCTIONS

Mix oil, eggs, sugar, and molasses. Sift together flour, salt, baking soda, and cinnamon. Stir into egg mixture. Separately, mix together oats, raisins, and nuts. Stir into dough. Drop by spoonfuls onto ungreased baking sheet. Bake 10 minutes at 400°.

# Brown Sugar Oatmeal Cookies

**Makes about 100 cookies**

## INGREDIENTS

- **4** cups shortening
- **5** cups brown sugar
- **½** cup honey
- **8** eggs
- **2** teaspoons vanilla
- **6** cups whole wheat flour
- **4** teaspoons baking soda
- **6** cups rolled oats
- **5** cups quick oats
- **2** teaspoons salt
- **4** cups raisins, chocolate chips, nuts, coconut (your choice how you divide these ingredients)

## INSTRUCTIONS

Mix all. Drop onto ungreased baking sheets by teaspoonful. Bake at 350° for 12–15 minutes.

# Cherry Triangles

**Makes about 2 dozen**

*One Saturday afternoon about a dozen of us girls were invited to my cousin and best friend Mary's house to a quilting. We all sat around her beautiful Wedding Ring quilt in the frame, stitching away, with our tongues probably moving faster than our needles.*

*I had told her I would bring something for our afternoon break and she said she'd make some kind of a special treat, too.*

*At around three o'clock, Mary's mom came in with a pitcher full of iced tea and a platter full of our goodies. We were all surprised that Mary and I had made the same thing! It was Cherry Triangles— mine were on half the platter and hers were on the other half. I was dismayed to see that hers were much bigger and lighter than mine! We couldn't figure out what had caused the difference, for we had used the same recipe. Then when she mentioned occident flour, I realized that I had used all-purpose flour instead! No wonder they had not risen like they should have! I was embarrassed, but haven't made the mistake of using the wrong flour since.*

## INGREDIENTS

- ¾ cup milk
- **1** cup butter
- **4** eggs, beaten
- **2** tablespoons active dry yeast
- ⅔ cup warm water
- ½ cup sugar
- **4½** cups occident flour
   cherry pie filling

## INSTRUCTIONS

Scald milk, remove from heat and cube butter into hot milk. When butter is melted, add beaten eggs. Put into large bowl. Put yeast in warm water. Add yeast, water, and sugar to milk mixture. Stir in flour. This is a soft dough and can't be kneaded. Refrigerate for several hours, then roll out into small squares on floured board. Put cherry pie filling on half the square, fold over to form a triangle, and seal. Cut small openings on top of each triangle for steam to escape. Place on greased baking sheets. Let rise for 1½ hour, covered with a kitchen towel, then bake at 350° for about 15 minutes, or until done.

# Chewy Molasses Cookies

**Makes about 6 dozen**

## INGREDIENTS

**2½** tablespoons baking soda

**½** cup boiling water

**1** pound raisins

**1½** cup water

**4⅔** cups white sugar

**2** cups margarine

**5** eggs, beaten

**1** teaspoon salt

**10** cups flour

**2** cups baking molasses

## INSTRUCTIONS

Put baking soda in boiling water and set aside. Grind or finely chop raisins. Place in saucepan with 1½ cup water and bring to boil. Cover and set aside to cool. Combine sugar, margarine, eggs, and salt. Add raisins and baking soda mixture to margarine mixture. Add rest of ingredients. Drop by spoonfuls onto ungreased cookie sheets, or make into rolls, refrigerate, and slice. Bake at 350° for 10–12 minutes.

# Delicious Whoopie Pies

**Makes about 8 dozen**

## INGREDIENTS

**2½** cups hot water

**3** tablespoons baking soda

**5** cups sugar

**9** cups bread flour

**2½** cups unsweetened cocoa powder

**1** teaspoon salt

**2½** cups vegetable oil

**5** eggs

**1½** tablespoon vanilla

**2½** cups buttermilk or sour milk

## INSTRUCTIONS

Mix the baking soda with the hot water and set aside. Mix rest of ingredients together, adding baking soda/water last. Drop by teaspoon onto greased baking sheets. Bake at 375° for 10–12 minutes. Make your favorite frosting and put 2 cookies together with frosting between them.

## Note

To make sour milk if you don't have buttermilk, add 1 teaspoon vinegar to 1 cup milk and let stand for a bit.

# Banana Waffle Whoopie Pies

**Makes 36 medium whoopie pies**

*Every time I make these whoopie pies, I remember the day I got the recipe. We had gone to help friends work on their house. They were building an addition and had put on a new roof, several feet higher than the old part.*

*We were making these waffle cookies when a shout was heard outside, at the north end of the house. One of the men came rushing inside, heading up the stairs, taking two steps at a time. We followed, reaching the top of the stairway in time to see him jump out the window and scramble up the old roof at the north end where a tarp was hung to close the gap between the new and old parts of the roof. He appeared again, holding his eighteen-month-old son.*

*From below he had seen the child crawling on the steep roof. Any misstep would have sent the child over the edge, falling about fourteen feet. The children had been playing upstairs, and he apparently had crawled onto the roof. The little fellow had slipped under the tarp and was out in the open on the eight-foot section of the old roof. The guardian angels must have been hovering close by that day!*

## INGREDIENTS

**2** eggs
**2** cups brown sugar
**½** cup vegetable oil
**1½** cup mashed banana
**1** teaspoon vanilla
**3** cups flour
**1** teaspoon baking powder
**1** teaspoon baking soda

## INSTRUCTIONS

Beat eggs until foamy. Add sugar, oil, banana, and vanilla. Stir in the dry ingredients. Bake in waffle pan according to manufacturer's directions, stopping to oil the waffle pan occasionally. Make your favorite frosting (cream cheese frosting recommended!) and put between 2 cooled waffle cookies.

# Chocolate Whoopie Pies

## Makes about 5 dozen whoopie pies

*My oldest sister used to bake chocolate and raisin oatmeal whoopie pies for a farm market. Usually there had to be at least fifty whoopie pies of each kind. Every Tuesday evening, we had to make a big batch of frosting. That took quite a bit of stirring, so we took turns until it was nice and creamy.*

*Every Wednesday morning was baking time. We liked whoopie-pie day, as sometimes we could get whoopie pies that cracked or were too big or something. Then in the afternoon, we took the nice whoopie pies about four miles to the market in the horse and buggy. The market was beside a busy highway and during the summer, a lot of tour buses stopped there. We usually met some tourists. Sometimes they were from a different country, and they liked to take pictures of us.*

### INGREDIENTS

**1** tablespoon baking soda

**1½** cup buttermilk

**3** whole eggs

**3** egg yolks

**3** cups brown sugar

**1½** cup shortening

**1½** teaspoon salt

**1** tablespoon vanilla

**1½** cup hot water

**1½** cup unsweetened cocoa powder

**5** cups flour

### INSTRUCTIONS

Dissolve baking soda in buttermilk. Mix rest of ingredients, adding buttermilk mixture last. Drop by spoonful onto greased baking sheets. Bake at 350° for 12–14 minutes, and cool. Fill with your favorite vanilla icing. Enjoy!

# Can't-Leave-Alone Bars

**Makes 1 (9 x 13-inch) pan**

## INGREDIENTS

**1** (16-ounce) white cake mix

**2** eggs

⅓ cup oil

¼ cup butter

**1** cup chocolate chips

**1** (14-ounce) can sweetened condensed milk

## INSTRUCTIONS

Mix together cake mix, eggs, and oil. Reserve ¾ cup crumbs. Pat remaining crumbs into 9 x 13-inch pan. Melt butter, chocolate chips, and sweetened condensed milk together until just combined. Pour on top of crumb crust in pan. Top with remaining crumb mixture by spoonfuls. Bake at 300° for 20–30 minutes.

# Lillian's Lemon Bars

**Makes 1 (9 x 13-inch) pan**

## INGREDIENTS

**1** (16-ounce) yellow cake mix

**1** egg, beaten

½ cup margarine

**1** (8-ounce) package cream cheese, room temperature

**3** eggs

**3** cups confectioners' sugar

**1** (3-ounce) package instant lemon pudding

## INSTRUCTIONS

Mix cake mix, beaten egg, and margarine together to make a thick batter. Set aside ¾ cup batter. Spread remaining batter in 9 x 13-inch pan. Beat cream cheese, eggs, confectioners' sugar, and pudding mix together. Pour over layer in pan and top with remaining batter, dropping evenly. Bake at 325° for 40 minutes.

# S'More Bars

## Makes 1 (7 x 11-inch) pan

*These are an all-around favorite, and my mom likes to make them for family gatherings. When my parents are busy with summer produce, my newlywed sister and I help out a day every week if we can. My brother's wife is always included, too. She blends right in with us. My little brothers and sisters are treated just like her own. Since she and my brother plan on moving out of state in a few years, we cherish the time we can spend with them now.*

*One day we planned to be together and, in fun, my sister-in-law told my little sisters to make those delicious granola bars to snack on that day. They knew she was teasing but decided to take her seriously anyway. Lo and behold, when we arrived, there stood a pan full of these tempting treats. My sister-in-law laughed a bit sheepishly, but by that evening, we had emptied the whole pan!*

### INGREDIENTS

**1** cup quick oats

½ cup flour

½ cup packed brown sugar

¼ teaspoon salt

¼ teaspoon baking soda

½ cup margarine, melted

**2** cups miniature marshmallows

½ cup chocolate chips

### INSTRUCTIONS

In a bowl, combine oats, flour, brown sugar, salt, and baking soda. Stir in margarine until crumbly. Press into a greased 7 x 11-inch baking dish. Bake at 350° for 10 minutes. Sprinkle with marshmallows and chocolate chips. Bake 5–7 minutes longer, or until marshmallows begin to brown. Cool on a wire rack. Cut into bars and enjoy!

# Marshmallow Bars

**Makes 1 (10 x 15-inch) pan**

*I still remember the first time I had Marshmallow Bars. It was about twenty years ago at the place I worked when I was a young girl. We always treated for our birthdays. I thought the Marshmallow Bars were simply delicious. Since then, I have made them quite often, and everyone always enjoys them.*

## INGREDIENTS

*Cake*

¾ cup butter or margarine

1½ cup sugar

3 eggs

1⅓ cup flour

1½ teaspoon baking powder

1½ teaspoon salt

3 tablespoons unsweetened cocoa powder

½ cup nuts, chopped

4 cups marshmallows

*Topping*

1⅓ cup (8 ounces) chocolate chips

3 tablespoons butter

1 cup peanut butter, chunky or smooth

2 cups crispy rice cereal

## INSTRUCTIONS

Mix cake ingredients all together (except for marshmallows) and bake in 10 x 15-inch jelly roll pan at 350° for 15 minutes. Sprinkle marshmallows evenly over hot cake and return to oven until they melt, 2–3 minutes. Use a knife dipped in water to spread melted marshmallows over cake. Make topping: Melt together chocolate chips, butter, and peanut butter until smooth. Add crispy rice cereal and spoon on top of marshmallow.

## Note

To make a white cake instead of a chocolate cake, use 3 tablespoons flour in place of cocoa.

# Coffee Bars

**Makes 1 (11 x 15-inch) pan**

*This is a quick and easy recipe that brings back memories of our newlywed days. A close friend and her husband lived nearby, and they were also just married.*

*One evening she invited me to come up for a while because both of our husbands had gone hunting and weren't back yet. When I walked in the door, she was baking Coffee Bars, which smelled absolutely delicious. Immediately, I asked for the recipe and she gave me a pen and paper so that I could make these yummy bars for my coffee-loving husband.*

*Now our friends have moved to a dairy farm, and we can't run up the road to them anymore. But we're still close friends and occasionally trade recipes. Precious memories remain, and our children will one day hear the stories behind the recipes we'll pass on to them!*

## INGREDIENTS

**2⅔** cups brown sugar
**3** cups flour
**1** cup cooking oil
**1** cup warm coffee
**2** eggs, beaten
**1** teaspoon salt
**1** teaspoon vanilla
**1** teaspoon baking soda
**1** cup nuts, chopped

*Topping*
**1** cup chocolate chips

## INSTRUCTIONS

Mix everything in a bowl and beat well. Pour into a greased 11 x 15-inch jelly roll pan and top with chocolate chips. Bake at 350° for 25–30 minutes.

**Optional:** Very good drizzled with coffee glaze on top after baking. Mix confectioners' sugar and a little bit of warm coffee to make a drizzle.

# Five-Star Brownies

**Makes 1 (9 x 13-inch) pan**

## INGREDIENTS

**3** eggs

**2** cups sugar

**1½** teaspoon vanilla extract

**½** cup butter or margarine, melted

**¼** cup shortening, melted

**1½** cup all-purpose flour

**¾** cup unsweetened cocoa powder

**1¼** teaspoon salt

**1** cup nuts, chopped; optional

## INSTRUCTIONS

In a mixing bowl, beat eggs, sugar, and vanilla until well mixed. Add butter and shortening. Combine flour, cocoa, and salt. Stir into egg mixture and mix well. Add nuts, if desired. Line a 9 x 13-inch pan with foil and grease the foil; pour batter into pan. Bake at 350° for 30 minutes, or until brownies test done with a wooden pick. Cool in pan. Turn brownies out of pan onto a cookie sheet. Remove foil. Cut into stars with a cookie cutter, or cut into bars.

# Chocolate Nut Brownies

**Makes 1 (7 x 11-inch) pan**

*We got this recipe from an English [non-Amish] couple. The man worked on the ambulance when my oldest brother was a baby and had to be taken to the hospital because of breathing problems. He was in serious condition, but the ambulance crew got him to the hospital in time. They got a gold medal pin because of their good work.*

*Now this man and his family always like to give my brother something for his birthday. The last couple of years, they brought vanilla ice cream with peanuts and chocolate syrup for the whole family. One time, they brought us two jars of chocolate nut brownie mix and the recipe for it. It then became a favorite brownie recipe among our family.*

## INGREDIENTS

*For jar*

**1**  cup + **2** tablespoons flour

⅔  cup brown sugar

⅓  cup unsweetened cocoa powder

½  cup chocolate chips

⅔  teaspoon salt

⅔  cup white sugar

½  cup shredded coconut

½  cup nuts, chopped

*To bake*

**3**  eggs

**1**  teaspoon vanilla

⅔  cup oil

## INSTRUCTIONS

Fill a quart jar with ingredients in order listed, but don't mix, because the layers look nice. When ready to bake, pour contents of jar into a bowl and whisk lightly. Add eggs, vanilla, and oil and mix well. Pour into a greased 7 x 11-inch pan. Bake at 350° for 25–30 minutes. Cool and cut into 2-inch squares.

# Chocolate Lover's Brownies

**Makes 1 (9 x 9-inch) pan**

*One evening we were alarmed to see an orange glow of flames in the night sky. The neighbor's barn, a mile west of us, was burning. Seconds later, we heard the wail of sirens and knew that help was on the way.*

*The neighbors quickly got together, hoping to be able to help. The women took along whatever they had on hand, knowing the firefighters would need refreshments. We had been planning to take hot lunch to school the next day and had made lots of cookies and bars. I took them along to the fire then instead. Others brought cheese and pretzels, and we made coffee and hot chocolate. The firefighters looked weary and beat when they came in for it, and several of them told us how much they appreciated it.*

## INGREDIENTS

- ¾ cup butter
- 1½ cup sugar
- 1 teaspoon vanilla
- 3 eggs
- ¾ cup flour
- ½ cup unsweetened cocoa powder
- ½ teaspoon baking powder
- ½ teaspoon salt

## INSTRUCTIONS

Melt butter. Add sugar, vanilla, and eggs. Beat. Set aside. Mix remaining ingredients and add to egg mixture. Pour into a greased 9 x 9-inch pan and bake at 325° for 30 minutes.

# Coconut Granola Bars

**Makes 1 (9 x 13-inch) pan**

*With three daughters to help me, our oldest son hardly gets a chance to bake. One Saturday he asked if he may make a pan of these bars. I copy recipes I'd like to try into a "scribbler"—appropriately named, as it sometimes gets pretty scribbly in there! I hadn't taken time to recopy this recipe and place it in my recipe box where the tried and good recipes eventually land. Near the "3" in ¾ cup sugar I had written "delicious," which partly covered up the "3." The results were a very sugary bar containing four cups of sugar and a disappointed baker!*

## INGREDIENTS

- ¾ cup brown sugar, packed
- ⅔ cup peanut butter
- ½ cup margarine, melted
- ½ cup corn syrup
- 2 teaspoons vanilla
- 1 cup chocolate chips
- ½ cup sunflower seeds
- 3 cups quick oats
- ½ cup flaked coconut
- ⅓ cup wheat germ
- 2 teaspoons sesame seeds

## INSTRUCTIONS

In a large bowl, combine brown sugar, peanut butter, margarine, corn syrup, and vanilla. Combine chocolate chips, sunflower seeds, oatmeal, coconut, and wheat germ, and add to peanut butter mixture. Stir to coat. Press into greased 9 x 13-inch pan. Sprinkle with sesame seeds. Bake at 350° for 25–30 minutes, or until golden brown. Cool and cut into bars.

# Anna's Granola Bars

**Makes 1 (9 x 13-inch) pan**

*This recipe comes from a mother who sent granola bars to school with her pupil for a birthday treat when I was teaching school. When I serve them to friends, they say they taste "musty" (must have more). Thus I keep passing the recipe on.*

## INGREDIENTS

¾  cup brown sugar

½  cup butter, melted

½  cup mild molasses

⅔  cup peanut butter

2  teaspoons vanilla

3  cups quick or rolled oats

⅓  cup wheat germ

½  cup raisins

½  cup sunflower seeds

½  cup chocolate chips

## INSTRUCTIONS

Mix brown sugar, butter, molasses, peanut butter, and vanilla. Add remaining ingredients. Stir. Press into a greased 9 x 13-inch pan. Bake 15 minutes at 350°.

Desserts
& Candy

# Peach Delight

**Serves 4–6**

*This recipe is very easy for little girls to make (I'm eight years old). When the others come in from milking our fifty cows, they are very happy to see that I made this peach dessert. It's really yummy with ice cream!*

### INGREDIENTS

- **5** fresh peaches
- **¾** cup quick oats
- **½** cup brown sugar
- **1** tablespoon flour
- **1** tablespoon butter

### INSTRUCTIONS

Slice peeled peaches and place in a greased 9-inch casserole dish or a large pie plate. Mix oats, brown sugar, flour, and butter into crumbs and sprinkle on top of peaches. Bake at 350° for 30 minutes, or until top is nicely browned. Serve warm with milk or ice cream.

# Blueberry Buckle

**Makes 1 (9-inch) pan**

### INGREDIENTS

- **¾** cup sugar
- **¼** cup margarine or butter
- **1** egg
- **½** cup milk
- **2** cups flour
- **2** teaspoons baking powder
- **½** teaspoon salt
- **2** cups fresh blueberries

*Topping*
- **½** cup sugar
- **⅓** cup flour
- **½** teaspoon cinnamon
- **¼** cup butter, softened

### INSTRUCTIONS

Mix sugar, margarine, and egg thoroughly. Stir in milk. Sift together flour, baking powder, and salt. Add to batter and mix well. Toss blueberries in a little flour and add them to batter. Spread into a greased and floured 9 x 9-inch square pan. Make topping by combining sugar, flour, and cinnamon. Add butter to make crumbs. Sprinkle over batter. Bake at 375° for 45–50 minutes.

# Fruit Cobbler

**Serves 4–6**

*I learned to make this while I was at my aunt and uncle's house when they had a new baby. My aunt was taking care of the baby and told me how to make it. Very simple!*

## INGREDIENTS

**1** quart fruit, peeled and chopped

**1¼** cup sugar, divided

**1** tablespoon tapioca, optional

**2** cups all-purpose flour

**2½** teaspoons baking powder

**½** teaspoon salt

**¼** cup oil

**¾** cup milk

**1** egg

butter, optional

cinnamon, optional

## INSTRUCTIONS

Put fruit (almost any kind works), ¼ cup sugar, and tapioca (if fruit has a lot of juice) in a large, greased baking pan. Stir together flour, 1 cup sugar, baking powder, and salt. Stir in oil, milk, and egg. Stir well and pour over the fruit. Dot with butter and sprinkle with cinnamon, if desired. Bake at 375° for 30 minutes. Serve warm with milk or ice cream. Delicious!

# Apple Crisp

**Serves 6**

## INGREDIENTS

**4** cups apples, sliced and pared

**¾** cup brown sugar, packed

**½** cup all-purpose flour

**¾** teaspoon cinnamon

**½** cup quick oats

**¾** teaspoon nutmeg

**⅓** cup margarine

## INSTRUCTIONS

Arrange apples in greased 9-inch pan. Mix remaining ingredients with a fork. Sprinkle over apples. Bake at 375° until apples are tender and topping is golden brown—about 30 minutes. Can be served with milk, cream, ice cream, or hard sauce, if desired.

# Ada's Apple Crunch

**Serves 6–8**

*Where we lived when we first were married, we had a small apple orchard. My favorite apples were those big, sweet ones we called Pound apples. I still get a longing to bite into one of those juicy, flavorful gems! The Yellow Delicious were best for canning apple pie filling and for drying. The flavor of the Red Delicious was hard to beat when they were at their peak, but all too soon they would turn mealy. The Stayman Winesap were best for winter eating. For our year's supply of applesauce, we used the tart Early Harvest apples, and sometimes the Summer Rambos. The Early Harvest needed more sugar than any other kind, but it was worth it. They all have their good points, though, and apples have always been my favorite fruit.*

## INGREDIENTS

8  apples, peeled and sliced
1  cup sugar
1  teaspoon cinnamon
⅛  teaspoon salt
¼  cup raisins

*Topping*
¾  cup rolled oats
¾  cup brown sugar
¼  cup butter, melted

## INSTRUCTIONS

Combine apples, sugar, cinnamon, salt, and raisins in greased casserole dish. Combine topping ingredients and pat on top of apples. Bake at 375° for 45 minutes.

# Grandpa's Apple Dumplings

**Serves 6**

*Years ago every fall, my brothers and older cousins got together to make firewood for Grandpa, who was a widower. We girls helped to stack the wood and had the job of making dinner for them. We were a close-knit family and always had a lot of fun on that day.*

*I remember one year a mischievous cousin let the billy goat out of his pen, and he ran into the orchard where we were working and butted my brother sharply in the behind. My brother was disgusted and figured out a way to get even. He thought of the story in our reading book at school. A billy goat greedily ate the biggest apple, and then was invited to an apple pie–party where his pie was filled with grass and he ran out the door, gagging.*

*We decided that "turn about is fair play," and we girls went along with my brother's plan when we made apple dumplings at Grandpa's house next fall. It sure was funny to see our cousin's face when he started eating his dumpling filled with grass! But we relented then, after we had our laugh, and gave him an actual apple dumpling.*

## INGREDIENTS

**6** medium-sized apples

**2** cups flour

**2½** teaspoons baking powder

**½** teaspoon salt

**⅔** cup margarine

**½** cup milk

  sugar

  cinnamon

*Sauce*

**2** cups brown sugar

**2** cups water

**¼** teaspoon cinnamon or nutmeg

**¼** cup butter

## INSTRUCTIONS

Pare and core apples, but leave whole. Mix flour, baking powder, and salt together. Cut in margarine until crumbly. Add milk and mix together lightly, working dough together. Roll dough into 6 squares. Place an apple on each. Fill cavity in apple with sugar and cinnamon. Wrap dough around apple. Place dumplings in baking pan. Make sauce: Combine brown sugar, water, and cinnamon or nutmeg. Cook 5 minutes. Add butter and stir until melted. Pour sauce over dumplings. Bake at 375° for 35–40 minutes. Serve hot with milk.

## Note

Apples could also be cut up and dough rolled out in a rectangle ¼ inch thick, with chopped apples spread over top. Roll up as a jelly roll. Cut into slices 1¼ inch thick. Place slices on baking pan. Cover with sauce.

# Fruit Pizza

**Serves 10**

One winter Mom was behind with making quilts for us girls for our hope chests, so we decided to hold a quilting. We girls invited all our friends on a Saturday and pinned two quilts into borrowed frames in the big sitting room. We had made this Fruit Pizza for an afternoon treat, along with coffee and tea. With all the lively chattering and storytelling, it sure was a lot more fun than doing the quilts alone.

Around midafternoon, Mom called us all out to the kitchen for the treat. My little two-year-old brother had already had his snack and wandered into the quilt room while we were eating out in the kitchen. He climbed up on a chair and crawled onto the quilt—the naughty little chap! The frame held up, but the quilt sagged way down, nearly to the floor, and he slid to the middle. The girls thought it was very funny and really laughed, but Mom and we girls couldn't see anything amusing about it. I don't think he ever tried that trick again!

## INGREDIENTS

*Crust*

**1½** cup flour

**1½** teaspoon baking powder

**½** cup sugar

**½** cup butter

**1½** tablespoon milk

**1½** teaspoon vanilla

*Topping*

**1** (8-ounce) package cream cheese, softened

**1** cup confectioners' sugar

**½** cup milk

**1** (3-ounce) box instant vanilla pudding

**8** ounces whipped topping

mandarin orange slices

pineapple, blueberries, and kiwi

**2** tablespoons strawberry gelatin

**2** tablespoons sugar

**1** tablespoon Clear Jel

## INSTRUCTIONS

Make crust: Combine flour, baking powder, and sugar. Cut in butter. Drizzle with milk and vanilla until dough forms. Press into a pizza pan. Bake at 350° for 10 minutes. Cool. Make topping: Mix cream cheese, confectioners' sugar, milk, and pudding mix. Add whipped topping and spread over cooled crust. Top with fruit. Combine gelatin, 2 tablespoons sugar, Clear Jel, and ¼ cup water, and cook just until thickened, stirring constantly. Cool and pour over fruit.

## Note

Fresh sliced strawberries may also be used with the glaze made with mashed strawberries, sugar, Clear Jel, and water. Add a little strawberry-flavored gelatin for color.

# Strawberry Pizza

**Serves 10**

## INGREDIENTS

- **1** cup flour
- **½** cup margarine
- **½** cup sugar
- **¼** cup confectioners' sugar
- **1** (8-ounce) package cream cheese, softened
- **1** quart strawberries, halved

*Glaze*
- **4** tablespoons sugar
- **4** tablespoons Clear Jel
- **1** cup berry juice

## INSTRUCTIONS

Cut together flour, margarine, and sugar to make crumbs. Sprinkle evenly over pizza pan. Press firmly. Bake at 325° for 12–15 minutes. Cool. Cream confectioners' sugar and cream cheese together and spread over cooled crust. Chill. Boil glaze ingredients together until thick. Cool. Arrange halved strawberries on cream cheese layer. Spread glaze over berries.

# Blueberry Delight

**Serves 6**

## INGREDIENTS

- **2** cups graham cracker crumbs
- **½** cup margarine, melted
- **2** cups confectioners' sugar
- **1** (8-ounce) package cream cheese, softened
- **8** ounces whipped topping
- **1** (21-ounce) can blueberry filling

## INSTRUCTIONS

Mix cracker crumbs with margarine and press into an 8 x 8-inch dish to make crust. Mix sugar with cream cheese and fold in topping. Pour mixture into cracker crust. Top with blueberry filling. Chill.

# Yoders' Eight-Minute Cheesecake

**Makes 1 (9-inch) pie**

*This eight-minute cheesecake is simply wonderful and very good. And very easy! It's a favorite among our family. I got it from a friend who I used to work for. She served it once for snack and since our family are big eaters, it really pays to make it.*

*Once when my sister came, I decided to make extra and sent some along home with her. And her family likes it too. It's different from the traditional kind because you don't have to bake it.*

## INGREDIENTS

- **8** ounces cream cheese, softened
- **⅓** cup sugar
- **1** cup sour cream
- **2** cups whipped topping
- **2** teaspoons vanilla
- **1** (9-inch) graham cracker pie crust
  pie filling or thickened fresh berries, to garnish

## INSTRUCTIONS

Beat cream cheese until smooth. Gradually beat in sugar. Stir in sour cream. Blend in whipped topping and vanilla. Spoon into cracker crust. Top with thickened strawberries, blackberries, raspberries, or cherries. Chill.

# Cherry Cheesecake

**Serves 12**

## INGREDIENTS

*Crust*
- **2** cups graham cracker crumbs
- **½** cup butter
- **¼** cup sugar

*Filling*
- **2** (8-ounce) packages cream cheese
- **2** eggs
- **2** cups sugar
- **2** teaspoons vanilla
  dash salt
- **2** (21-ounce) cans cherry pie filling

## INSTRUCTIONS

Combine crust ingredients. Press into 9-inch springform pan. Blend cream cheese, eggs, sugar, vanilla, and salt. Spread over crust and bake for 20 minutes at 350°. Cool. Top with cherry pie filling. Refrigerate 2 hours.

# Cottage Puffs Dessert

**Serves 8**

*When I was twelve years old, we moved to a new settlement where we were the first Amish. I can well remember the lonely feeling the first Sunday of being the only Amish people living here. I got the mumps a day or two after we moved, so I had some unhappy, lonely days while the rest went out and cut trees and cleaned up.*

*We only had a house and a little shed for a barn. That first summer we built a barn. One day while the men were helping, we made these Cottage Puffs for a treat. One of the men went home and told his wife to get the recipe for those "little black things" they had. And that's what some people call them. We often make them for a quick company dessert.*

## INGREDIENTS

*Puffs*

⅔ cup white sugar

¼ cup oil

**1** egg

**1** teaspoon vanilla

**1** cup milk

2½ cups pastry flour

**4** teaspoons baking powder

½ teaspoon salt

*Sauce*

**2** tablespoons cornstarch

½ cup unsweetened cocoa powder

**1** cup white sugar

**1** teaspoon vanilla

pinch salt

1½ cup water, divided

## INSTRUCTIONS

Make puffs: Mix together all ingredients. Fill well-greased cupcake pans half full with batter, for a total of about 16 puffs. Bake at 350° for about 15 minutes. While still warm, remove from cupcake pans and place in two deep bowls. Make sauce: Put cornstarch, cocoa, sugar, vanilla, and salt in saucepan. Add ½ cup cold water and mix until smooth. Add 1 cup boiling water and stir over low heat until thickened. Pour over the puffs in the bowl and serve hot.

## Note

Wonderful with some fresh strawberries or raspberries on top!

# Peanut Butter Dessert

**Serves 6**

*This is a rich dessert for special occasions. One memory we have of this dessert is from my sister's husband, who really likes peanut butter. He had surgery this past spring. Although he had a swift recovery, he had little appetite and lost a lot of weight. So I whipped together this dessert to take along when we went to visit. My sister told us later how much he ate and wished we had brought more. We were glad he liked it and figured all those calories were just what he needed to regain those lost pounds! As of now, he's back to work and looks so healthy you would never know how sick he had been. Praise God for his healing power and for blessing us with plenty of food to eat.*

## INGREDIENTS

- **1** (8-ounce) package cream cheese
- **1** cup confectioners' sugar
- **½** cup peanut butter
- **½** cup milk
- **1** (8-ounce) container whipped topping

  Oreo cookie crumbs

## INSTRUCTIONS

Mix cream cheese, sugar, peanut butter, and milk together. Stir in whipped topping. Line the bottom of a dessert dish with Oreo cookie crumbs. Add pudding mixture, putting some Oreo crumbs on top. Refrigerate to firm up. Enjoy!

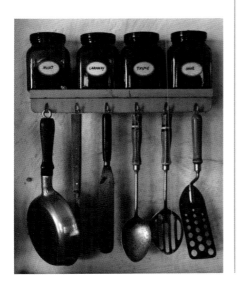

# Éclair Dessert

**Serves 12**

When I was a young girl going to school in our one-room country school, the teacher presented the idea of a "guinea pig" dinner. Each older girl student would make a part of the meal, using a recipe they never made alone before—the reason it was called "guinea pig." We were all for it.

I decided on Éclair Dessert, and I started off with high spirits and a clean sink. Mom helped me scald the milk, because I was a little scared of trying that alone the first time I did it. Everything went fine—to my way of thinking—and I carefully transported it to school.

When lunch was served to excited pupils, some of them commented how "chocolate-y" my dessert was! I gave it no thought until that evening when my family had the leftovers for supper. Mom exclaimed, "It's so strong, how much cocoa did you use?"

"Three cups," I answered so assuredly.

"Oh my!" she gasped. "Didn't you see the recipe says three tablespoons?"

My brothers nicknamed that dessert "Black Top."

## INGREDIENTS

- **¾–1** pound graham crackers
- **2** (3-ounce) packages French vanilla or vanilla instant pudding
- **3½** cups milk, scalded and cooled
- **9** ounces whipped topping, or 1 cup whipping cream, whipped

*Topping*

- **3** tablespoons unsweetened cocoa powder
- **2** tablespoons oil
- **2** teaspoons white Karo syrup
- **2** teaspoons vanilla
- **3** tablespoons soft margarine
- **1½** cup confectioners' sugar
- **1** tablespoon milk

## INSTRUCTIONS

Line bottom of a 9 x 13-inch pan with graham crackers. Beat instant pudding and milk together. Blend well and fold in whipped topping. Spread half on crackers. Add another layers of crackers, the rest of the pudding, and a final layer of crackers. Beat together topping ingredients. Spread over top layer of crackers. Refrigerate for at least 24 hours before serving.

## Notes

If you must use raw milk, bring it to a boil first and cool until cold. For variety, use black cherry pie filling instead of chocolate topping.

# Fancy Four-Layer Dessert

**Makes 1 (9 x 13-inch) pan**

*This is one of our favorite desserts now, but almost every time I serve it, I think of the proverb "Pride goeth before a fall." I was newly married and wanted to make something extra special for dessert. I believe I was trying to impress my husband that I'm a good cook. It turned out well, and I was patting myself on the back, really pleased that I had something good to offer him. His two little sisters, ages three and four, came over for supper that evening, and after we had finished our first course, I went to the refrigerator for my showpiece. I don't know how it happened, but as I was lifting it out, it slipped out of my grasp and crashed to the floor, breaking the glass dish. Hubby was very sympathetic and helped to scoop it up into another dish, declaring that what hadn't touched the floor was still fit to eat. The dish had merely cracked in two, and we thought there were no glass chips. Imagine my horror when the three-year-old spat out a big glass chip when eating some of the dessert. We quickly removed the rest of it from the table, thankful she wasn't cut and hadn't swallowed the glass.*

*I think I learned two lessons there—pride goeth before a fall, and never eat anything from a broken dish.*

## INGREDIENTS

*Crust*

**1½** cup flour

**¾** cup butter

**½–1** cup pecans, chopped

*Second layer*

**1** (8-ounce) package cream cheese, softened

**1** cup whipped cream

**1** cup confectioners' sugar

*Third layer*

**2** (3-ounce) packages instant butterscotch, lemon, or chocolate pudding mix

**3** cups cold milk

*Fourth layer*

whipped topping or whipped cream

chopped nuts or candy bars, optional

## INSTRUCTIONS

Mix crust ingredients and press into the bottom of a 9 x 13-inch pan. Bake at 350° for 15 minutes. Combine cream cheese, whipped cream, and confectioners' sugar; spread on cooled crust. Prepare pudding mix with cold milk, and spread on top of second layer. Top with whipped topping and sprinkle with chopped nuts. Chill.

# Cherry Dessert

**Makes 8 cups**

*Copying this recipe reminded me of when I was of preschool age and had a little table and two chairs just my size. I used to carry it out under the apple tree and have a little tea party with my dolls. Mother let me have tea for the cups, and animal crackers and raisins for the plates. What fun it was to pretend to be grown-up and having visitors!*

*Once when it was my birthday, Mother made Cherry Dessert for the occasion. She helped me to wash and dry my tea set, then joined me for my tea party on the lawn. We ate the Cherry Dessert off my little plates with the tiny spoons. What fun that was! I remember pretending to be Aunt Lydia, and Mother and I had a very interesting grown-up chat.*

### INGREDIENTS

**1** (14-ounce) can sweetened condensed milk

**¼** cup lemon juice

**1** (15-ounce) can crushed pineapple, well-drained

**1** (21-ounce) can cherry pie filling

**16** ounces whipped topping

### INSTRUCTIONS

Mix sweetened condensed milk and lemon juice together. Beat. Add pineapple and pie filling. Fold in whipped topping and chill overnight before serving.

# Rhubarb Dessert

**Serves 8**

*When we got married twenty-one years ago, a friend of my mother's gave me this recipe. Every spring when rhubarb is in season, we eat a lot of this dessert. It's simple to make and very delicious.*

### INGREDIENTS

**4** cups rhubarb, chopped

**4½** cups water

**2** cups sugar

**½** cup fine tapioca

**¾** cup strawberry gelatin

### INSTRUCTIONS

Cook rhubarb, water, sugar, and tapioca together until the tapioca is clear. Then add gelatin. Chill. It will thicken in the refrigerator.

# Fruit Cocktail

**Serves 6**

## INGREDIENTS

- **1** (20-ounce) can pineapple
- **1** tablespoon butter
- **½** cup sugar
- **1** egg, beaten
- **1** tablespoon flour
- **1** cup whipped cream
- **1** dozen large marshmallows, or 2 cups mini marshmallows
- **1–2** oranges
- **6** bananas

## INSTRUCTIONS

Drain juice from pineapple. Add butter, sugar, egg, and flour. Cook until thickened. When cool, fold in whipped cream. Mix together marshmallows, pineapples, oranges, and bananas in nice dessert bowl. Pour sauce over fruit.

# Peach Pudding Delight

**Serves 8**

## INGREDIENTS

- **4** cups hot vanilla pudding
- **½** cup peach-flavored gelatin
- **12** ounces whipped topping
- **1** cup sugar
- **3** tablespoons instant Clear Jel
- **4** cups fresh peaches, diced and peeled

## INSTRUCTIONS

Make your favorite vanilla pudding. Remove from heat, add gelatin to hot pudding. When cool, but not set, add whipped topping. Put in dessert dish. Mix sugar and instant Clear Jel. Add to peaches and put on top of the pudding. Chill.

# Grape Sponge

**Serves 4–6**

*Grape Sponge was one of my mother's favorites. Every fall when the grapes were ripe, she would make this recipe.*

*She has gone on to that Better Land, and I miss her so. My first memories of her were of being rocked to sleep and of sitting in church with my head resting in her lap. Sitting beside her in the carriage on the way to church, I knew my face had better be clean, or she'd wet the corner of her hankie and scrub away!*

*On Sunday evenings, she'd get us all into going for a walk. We'd gather bouquets of wildflowers, something I still love to do. We'd see if we could catch a glimpse of those tiny spring peepers.*

*In the winter, she'd get out the boxes of fabric scraps and we had many an evening of cutting and sewing. First she had me make a four-patch quilt, and then a nine-patch. When I sewed wrong, she taught me how to rip it open and try again. How I detested that, but I'm so glad now to have been taught!*

*How proud I was of the first cake she helped me to make. In cooking she taught me to keep it simple and healthy, something I still try to follow.*

## INGREDIENTS

- **1** tablespoon unflavored gelatin
- **½** cup cold water
- **1** cup hot grape juice
- **½** cup sugar
- **2** tablespoons lemon juice
- **1½** cup whipped topping

## INSTRUCTIONS

Soften gelatin in cold water. Stir in hot grape juice, sugar, and lemon juice. Cool. Stir occasionally. When it begins to set, beat with a rotary beater until frothy. Beat in whipped topping and continue beating until mixture holds its shape. Pile in sherbet glasses. Chill. Serve with soft custard as sauce.

# Pumpkin Custard

**Serves 4**

*The other week I baked Pumpkin Custard from the pumpkins I raise. My youngest brother, age six, declared right away before he barely tasted it that he didn't like it. He was the only one, though: everyone else loved it!*

### INGREDIENTS

**2** eggs, separated

**2** cups mashed pumpkin

**1** cup plain bread crumbs

**1½** cup milk

**¼** teaspoon salt

**1** teaspoon orange extract

**1** cup brown sugar

**1** tablespoon butter

### INSTRUCTIONS

Beat egg whites until stiff. Mix rest of ingredients together, folding in egg whites last. Pour into greased 1½-quart casserole dish. Bake at 360° until custard is set, about 30 minutes. Chill, then serve with whipped cream.

### Note

May reserve egg whites for meringue on top and skip the whipped cream.

# Coffee Carnival

**Serves 4–6**

*I first enjoyed this recipe at a friend's house. I never learned to drink coffee, but this and coffee ice cream gave me an appetite for it. I usually use milk instead of water to make it, as I always have plenty of milk on hand.*

### INGREDIENTS

**½** cup minute tapioca

**½** teaspoon salt

**⅓** cup raisins

**½** cup sugar

**1½** cup milk or water

**1** cup strong coffee

**1** teaspoon vanilla

**1** cup whipped cream

### INSTRUCTIONS

Mix tapioca, salt, raisins, sugar, and milk in heavy saucepan. Boil several minutes, stirring constantly. Remove from heat and add coffee and vanilla. Cool, stirring occasionally. Chill. Fold in whipped cream.

# Butterscotch Tapioca

**Serves 10**

We had company one day in the summer a few years ago. Men were helping put new windows and siding on the house. The women were talking and helping with dinner. With all the sawing and hammering going on, it was hard to concentrate. The flies were coming in and were often a mess to sweep away. I was asked to cook some tapioca in the midst of this.

After heating the stove, I stirred and waited for quite a while and still nothing happened. Not knowing what else to do, I got Mom to check on it. Taking a close look, she discovered I had fine coconut in there instead of minute tapioca! What embarrassment. To this day, I'm still being reminded of my "Coconut Tapioca."

## INGREDIENTS

- **6** cups water
- **1½** cup granulated or small pearl tapioca
- **2** cups brown sugar
- **½** cup white sugar
- **2** eggs, beaten
- **1** cup milk
- **1** teaspoon salt
- **1** teaspoon vanilla
- **½** cup butter
- **2** cups whipped cream
- **4** butterscotch candy bars, chopped

## INSTRUCTIONS

Bring to boil, stirring often, water, tapioca, both sugars, eggs, milk, and salt. Boil for 3 minutes. Add vanilla and set aside. Separately, brown the butter. Add to pudding. Cool. Top with cream and candy bars.

# Graham Cracker Fluff

**Serves 4–6**

*The Graham Cracker Fluff you will want to try if you haven't yet. It's a very old recipe that everyone should like.*

*I remember when I was small, we children liked it so well that one Christmas morning as we sat down to eat breakfast, my mother came with a bowl of the good yellow shimmering fluff for each of us. We each had a whole bowl to ourselves and could eat it whenever we wanted. That sure was a treat!*

## INGREDIENTS

**1½** teaspoon unflavored gelatin

**⅓** cup cold water

**½** cup sugar

**¾** cup whole milk

**2** egg yolks

**1** teaspoon vanilla

**2** egg whites, stiffly beaten

**1** cup whipped cream

**1½** tablespoon butter

**3** tablespoons brown sugar

**12** graham crackers, crushed

## INSTRUCTIONS

Soak gelatin in cold water and set aside. Mix sugar, milk, and egg yolks in a saucepan. Cook for 1 minute, stirring all the time. Remove from heat. Add gelatin and vanilla. Chill until mixture begins to thicken, then add stiffly beaten egg whites and whipped cream. Chill while making crumbs. Melt butter and brown sugar together. Mix with crushed graham crackers. Line bottom of dish with half of crumbs and pour in pudding. Put remaining crumbs on top. Chill. Delicious!

# Grandma's Caramel Pudding

**Serves 6**

*This recipe was a favorite while I was growing up. It brings back memories of going to Grandma's, for this was what she often served for dessert. When Grandma passed this recipe on to my mom, she had no written recipe—she just told Mom the way she did it and Mom wrote it down so she could pass it on to us girls, too.*

*I remember when we were little girls and Mom was making this pudding how we liked to eat a bit of the caramelized browned sugars and butter before she stirred in the milk. Of course, Mom didn't let us take too much or it would have spoiled the pudding.*

*When Mom invited company for a meal, she was almost always sure to serve this pudding. We lived on a dairy farm and she had all the milk she needed. My husband and I also served this pudding at our wedding—we made ten portions of it!*

## INGREDIENTS

¾ cup brown sugar

½ cup white sugar

¼ cup butter

6 cups milk, divided

2 heaping tablespoons cornstarch

1 tablespoon Clear Jel

1 egg

½ teaspoon salt

1 teaspoon vanilla

## INSTRUCTIONS

Melt brown sugar, white sugar, and butter in a saucepan and brown it to caramel color. Add 5 cups milk. Bring to almost boiling point. Combine cornstarch, Clear Jel, egg, and salt into the reserved 1 cup milk. Mix to a smooth paste and stir into the hot mixture. Cook until thickened, then add vanilla. Chill before serving.

# Caramel Maple Pudding

**Serves 4–6**

*I had a memorable time making this pudding once. I had everything added already and was cooking it in the dutch oven on the stovetop. All of a sudden, I heard a clattering sound and "Whoa! Whoa! Whoa!" I ran to the window and saw our pony hitched to the cart, running out the lane. He was galloping at top speed and the cart was bouncing up and down. He hit a rock by the roadside and the seat flew off and landed in the gutter. At the next bump, the pony cart overturned and was dragging along. Our neighbor caught him at the end of his lane and brought him back. Not until the excitement was all over did I think of my pudding. The bottom was so scorched that the taste went all the way through it, and I had to make another go. Hope you have better luck!*

## INGREDIENTS

- ¾ cup brown sugar
- ¼ cup water
- ¼ teaspoon salt
- 4 cups milk
- ⅓ cup cornstarch
- 2 tablespoons butter
- 1 teaspoon maple flavoring

## INSTRUCTIONS

Cook sugar, water, and salt until slightly browned. Stir together milk and cornstarch and pour into sugar mixture. Cook until thickened. Remove from heat and stir in butter and maple flavoring. Pour into nice glass dish. Cool. Good served with sweetened whipped cream.

# Easy Butterscotch Pudding

**Serves 8**

At school, we made a little recipe book for a Mother's Day gift. Everyone had to bring a recipe along to put in. That's where we got this recipe, and have used it a lot since. That page is all smeared with brown blotches, and all tattered, but it still serves the purpose. It was the beginner's pudding recipe for my sisters and me because it's so easy to make.

It's also our number one pudding for company dinners. We have goats for our milk supply. Friends who are accustomed to cow's milk find it a bit different tasting, but with this pudding, they take second helpings, and afterward ask for the recipe!

## INGREDIENTS

**1½–2** quarts milk

**1** cup mild molasses

**1** cup brown sugar

**1** cup flour

**½** cup butter

**1** tablespoon vanilla

**5** eggs

## INSTRUCTIONS

In a heavy kettle, bring milk to boiling. Beat rest of ingredients together and add to hot milk. Stir constantly until pudding is thick. Cool and top with your favorite topping.

# Vanilla Ice Cream

**Serves 15–20**

When I was a girl, I had a favorite spot to sit and read or to go to when I just wanted to be alone. It was a wide branch up in an apple tree between the chicken house and the meadow fence. From there I could see the back part of the house and the comings and goings of the others, and I was within calling distance of the back door.

One Saturday afternoon, on a lovely spring day when the apple tree was in blossom and the robins were singing, I was sitting up there reading and enjoying the fragrance and beauty of the blossoms. The back door opened and I heard my older sister call me. I didn't want to go help finish the cleaning; there were just the porches and walks to do yet, and I figured she could do that, so I pretended I hadn't heard. After a while she went back inside, and I happily went on reading.

About an hour later, I climbed down and sauntered back to the house, feeling a little guilty. What a disappointment I had when they told me that our favorite single aunt had been there (she came in the front door) and had brought homemade ice cream! I felt like crying (and did too, later). I was sorry I didn't get to taste the ice cream and sorrier yet that I didn't get to talk to my aunt.

But I learned a good lesson from it—and later got her ice cream recipe. But nothing ever really tastes as special as when you eat it with loved ones.

## INGREDIENTS

**1¼** quart milk

**2** (12-ounce) cans evaporated milk

**5** eggs, slightly beaten

**¾** cup white sugar

**1** cup brown sugar

**7** tablespoons cornstarch

   dash salt

**1** (14-ounce) can sweetened condensed milk

**1** tablespoon vanilla

## INSTRUCTIONS

Heat the milk and evaporated milk to boiling. Mix beaten eggs, sugars, cornstarch, and salt. Beat well. Add to the boiling milk and cook to boiling again. Remove from heat. Add sweetened condensed milk and vanilla. Cool. Freeze in ice cream freezer.

# Velvet Ice Cream

**Makes 6 quarts**

*This ice cream is a favorite of ours. It doesn't have that "floury burnt" taste that boiled ice cream often has. I remember noticing that as a child when we went to neighborhood gatherings.*

*This recipe seems to make better ice cream if the pudding is on the thin side. The can should be fairly full before starting to freeze it, being as the cream and egg whites are whipped.*

*We all enjoy our homemade ice cream. After all, what is more rewarding on a warm day?*

## INGREDIENTS

- **9** cups milk, divided
- **2** cups sugar, white or brown
- **4½** tablespoons cornstarch
- **7** egg yolks
- **7** egg whites, stiffly beaten
- **½** teaspoon salt
- **½** teaspoon maple flavor
- **3** cups heavy cream, whipped

## INSTRUCTIONS

Heat 8 cups milk to scalding. Mix sugar with cornstarch and egg yolks with remaining 1 cup milk. Add to the hot milk. Stir until it thickens. Fold in egg whites. Remove from heat. Add salt and flavoring. Cool. Fold in the whipped cream. Freeze in ice cream freezer.

# Strawberry Ice Cream

**Makes 4 quarts**

## INGREDIENTS

- **4** cups sugar
- **¾** cup instant Clear Jel
- **2** cups crushed strawberries
- **3** quarts milk
- **2** cups cream

## INSTRUCTIONS

Mix sugar and instant Clear Jel, then mix into the berries. Mix it with milk and cream in a 6- or 8-quart ice cream freezer. Freeze and enjoy!

# Peppermint Twirl Ice Cream

**Makes 4 quarts**

*One day we had a special Valentine's Day party at school. The teacher served pink iced heart-shaped cookies; strawberry-flavored, heart-shaped finger Jell-O; and valentine candies.*

*Best of all, she had her brother bring the ingredients for Peppermint Twirl Ice Cream at last recess! The girls helped to get it ready and the boys cranked the freezer. When it was ready, we dipped it into ice cream cones, and we all thought it was the most delicious we'd ever tasted. I still make it often.*

*We passed out the valentines then, which were much prettier than the ones they have nowadays because they were homemade.*

### INGREDIENTS

**4** cups milk

**2** cups sugar

**¼** teaspoon salt

**2** quarts cream

**2** teaspoons vanilla

**3** cups peppermint twirl candies, finely crushed

### INSTRUCTIONS

Scald milk; add sugar and salt. Stir until dissolved. Add cream and vanilla. Chill. Freeze in the ice cream freezer. Crush candy in blender in 4 batches. Add after the ice cream is frozen but not hardened.

# Peach Ice Cream

**Makes 3 quarts**

### INGREDIENTS

**4** cups fresh peaches, peeled and diced

**1½** cup sugar

**2** cups heavy cream

**4** cups milk

**1** teaspoon vanilla

**1** teaspoon lemon juice

**½** teaspoon salt

### INSTRUCTIONS

Mix peaches and sugar and let stand 30 minutes. Add remaining ingredients and freeze in 4-quart ice cream freezer. Enjoy!

# Coffee Ice Cream

*Several folks were helping my sister and her husband with a building project. After supper, they enjoyed a bedtime snack of Coffee Ice Cream, not thinking that it's not a good bedtime snack for some people. Some of them could not fall asleep when they wanted to because of the coffee! There were some very tired workers the next day.*

### INGREDIENTS

- **8** cups whole milk, divided
- **4** eggs, beaten
- **1** cup strong, cold coffee
- **1** cup sweet cream
- **1½** cup sugar
- **⅔** cup instant Clear Jel

### INSTRUCTIONS

Put 1 cup milk in a saucepan, add the 4 beaten eggs and simmer for several minutes. Mix remaining 7 cups milk, coffee, and cream and add to egg mixture. Chill. Mix sugar and Clear Jel. Add to chilled coffee mixture and beat well. Pour into ice cream mixer and churn.

# Raspberry Sherbet

**Serves 4**

### INGREDIENTS

- **1** cup water
- **½** cup sugar
- **3** ounces raspberry gelatin
- **1** tablespoon lemon juice
- **2½** cups milk

### INSTRUCTIONS

Boil water and sugar 1 minute. Add gelatin. Cool. Stir in lemon juice and milk. Freeze 1 hour. Beat well and enjoy!

# Southern Buckeyes

**Makes about 5 dozen**

*On my fourteenth birthday, we woke up to find out that about two feet of snow had fallen during the night, and the wind was whistling all around the corners of the house and barn. That meant no school. I wanted to do something special because it was my birthday. Mother said I could sew a new apron for myself and make any kind of candy I wished.*

*It was just a week before Christmas, and I had a hard time deciding which kind of candy I wanted to make, for they all sounded so good. I ended up making three different kinds.*

## INGREDIENTS

**1** pound peanut butter

**1½** pound confectioners' sugar

**1** pound butter

**¼** cup ground walnuts

**¼** cup finely diced dates

**1** (12-ounce) package chocolate chips

**½** stick paraffin

## INSTRUCTIONS

Mix peanut butter and confectioners' sugar. Then add butter, walnuts, and dates. Roll into balls and let chill thoroughly. Melt chocolate chips and paraffin. Dip the balls in this.

# No-Bake Treats

**Makes about 3 dozen**

*No-Bake Treats are a very special snack at our house! We do consider them candy more than cookies, and have made them for school treats, family gatherings, gifts, and picnics. They always seem to be a favorite of others, too.*

### INGREDIENTS

**2** cups sugar

**3** tablespoons unsweetened cocoa powder

**¼** cup water

**½** cup milk

**3** cups quick oats

**½** cup peanut butter

**1** teaspoon vanilla

### INSTRUCTIONS

Boil sugar, cocoa, water, and milk for 1 minute. Remove from heat. Add remaining ingredients. Drop quickly onto waxed paper by teaspoonfuls.

### Notes

Coconut, nuts, or chocolate chips may be used instead of peanut butter. May use half old-fashioned rolled oats or chunky peanut butter for more texture.

# Peanut Butter Creams

**Makes 2–3 dozen**

### INGREDIENTS

**1** pound confectioners' sugar

**¼** teaspoon salt

**1** teaspoon vanilla

**2** cups peanut butter

**4** tablespoons butter, softened

**3** tablespoons water, more if dry
   chocolate, melted

### INSTRUCTIONS

Mix until candy forms a smooth dough. Shape into small balls and dip in melted chocolate.

# Peanut Butter Fudge

**Makes 1 (9-inch) pan**

*I got this recipe from a friend last Christmas. Fifteen of us cousins and friends had gone caroling on Christmas Eve evening. We had been hoping so much for snow so we could use the big bobsled, but the weather didn't cooperate. Instead, my brother hitched the two workhorses to the big flat wagon and attached bells to the harnesses, and we all piled on.*

*The bells were jingling merrily as the horses clopped from house to house, to the elderly and shut-ins. We sang for a good friend of ours who had been in an accident some time before and was recuperating. She served us this Peanut Butter Fudge along with hot chocolate and cookies cut into star and bell shapes and frosted with red-tinted sugar. We all enjoyed spreading Christmas joy and cheer, even though it didn't snow.*

### INGREDIENTS

⅔ cup evaporated milk
2 cups sugar
1 cup peanut butter
1 cup marshmallow crème
1 teaspoon vanilla

### INSTRUCTIONS

Grease sides of a 2-quart saucepan. Combine sugar and milk in pan. Stir over medium heat. Boil to soft-ball stage (235°). Remove from heat and add peanut butter, marshmallow crème, and vanilla. Stir until well blended. Pour into 9 x 9-inch pan. Cut when firm.

# Crispy Butterscotch Candy

**Serves 10**

### INGREDIENTS

¼ cup butter
32 large marshmallows
5 cups crispy rice cereal
1 cup butterscotch chips

### INSTRUCTIONS

Melt butter and marshmallow in saucepan, stirring constantly. Keep stirring it. Pour it over crispy rice cereal and butterscotch chips. Mix. Pack into a buttered container. Cut into squares.

Snacks,
Beverages,
& Extras

# Vanilla Popcorn

**Makes 3 quarts**

*It was late one dark night—the children were in bed, and I was waiting for my husband to come home. He is rarely away evenings, so I minded the quiet and the dark. After a while, the silence was broken with an unusual sound—a sound like hail pebbling on a tin roof. And it was coming from the almost empty popcorn bowl on the counter.*

*With great apprehension, I peeked into the bowl. A poor little mouse with buttered paws was frantically trying to escape. Its frenzied attempts kicked kernels against the sides, creating quite a rattle (it must have felt like I do some days!).*

*I carefully picked up the bowl and put it outside. Two of our cats were out there and one got a treat, because they don't share. And the bowl got soaked in bleach all night long!*

## INGREDIENTS

- **3** quarts popped popcorn
- **1** cup sugar
- **½** cup butter
- **¼** cup light corn syrup
- **¼** teaspoon baking soda
- **½** teaspoon vanilla

## INSTRUCTIONS

Place popcorn in a large bowl. In a saucepan, combine sugar, butter, corn syrup, and baking soda. Bring to a boil over medium heat. Boil and stir until mixture is golden—about 2 minutes. Remove from heat, stir in vanilla. Pour over popcorn and toss to coat. Cool slightly and break apart while warm.

# Party Popcorn Balls

**Serves 6–8**

When I was a child, on Christmas Day, we always had a surprise beside our plate at the breakfast table—a small handmade gift such as new mittens, crochet-edged handkerchiefs, scarves, etc. Also, always a small dish of hard candy and an orange. This was very special to us, for we never had store-bought candy at any other time. So we made it last a long time, and also savored every bit of that orange.

When I had a family of my own, I continued that tradition and included a big popcorn ball at each plate, too. There were also bigger gifts later in the day when the cousins, aunts, and uncles got together for the Christmas dinner. My mother always made sure that all the children and grandchildren were aware of the real meaning of Christmas, and Dad would read aloud the Christmas story to us all after dinner.

### INGREDIENTS

**½** cup white corn syrup

**1** cup butter

**1** teaspoon vanilla

**1⅓** cup sugar

**2½** quarts popped popcorn

**2** cups peanuts

### INSTRUCTIONS

Cook corn syrup, butter, vanilla, and sugar for 10–15 minutes to hard-ball stage (250°–266°). Pour over popcorn and peanuts, and shape into balls.

# Pretzel and Chip Dip

**Makes 3½ cups**

### INGREDIENTS

**2** cups mayonnaise

**1½** cup sour cream

**½** teaspoon onion salt

**½** teaspoon garlic salt

**1½** teaspoon parsley flakes

### INSTRUCTIONS

Mix all together and store in refrigerator. Serve with celery and carrot sticks, pretzels, or potato chips. Delicious!

# Slush Punch

**Serves 8**

*Our next-door neighbors had their sixth child a week after we had our first, Kristina. That first summer it was very humid for long periods of time. The neighbor girl kept Kristina with her baby boy while I helped them pick tomatoes. She thought that was a fair deal, and I enjoyed working outside. She introduced me to this refreshing drink, and I have enjoyed preparing it on warm summer days since.*

*I don't always have everything on hand, so it's an extra-special treat we appreciate in humid weather.*

### INGREDIENTS

- **1** cup strawberry gelatin
- **2** cups boiling water
- **1** cup sugar
- **1** (6-ounce) can frozen orange juice concentrate
- **1** (46-ounce) can pineapple juice
- **6** cups cold water
- **2** quarts ginger ale

### INSTRUCTIONS

Dissolve gelatin in boiling water, then add sugar, both juices, and cold water. Freeze 1–2 hours before use—remove and let stand until slightly slushy. Pour 2 quarts ginger ale over it or fill tumblers with half ginger ale and half slush.

# Four-Hour Root Beer

**Makes 1 gallon**

### INGREDIENTS

- **2** cups sugar
- **4** teaspoons root beer extract
- **1** teaspoon active dry yeast
  lukewarm water

### INSTRUCTIONS

Mix sugar with root beer extract. Mix yeast with a little lukewarm water. Add almost a gallon of lukewarm water to the sugar mixture, then add the yeast. Set in the sun upright for 4 hours. Don't turn the lid on tight!

# Homemade Tea Concentrate

**Makes 1 gallon concentrate (3 gallons tea)**

*What is more fragrant than the first meadow tea that grows along country lanes, meadows, and in our garden tea patch in the spring? Whenever I go for a stroll in the evening, when twilight is descending and the birds sweetly singing, or go to fetch the cow in the morning when everything is fresh and sparkling with dew, I can't resist picking a handful of the tea leaves, just to breathe in the sweet deliciousness of them. I love icy cold glassfuls of that good tea when I come in hot and thirsty from hoeing in the garden or pushing the clattering reel mower. It sure is better than any store-bought variety!*

*Years ago I heard a preacher remark that people are like tea leaves: their real flavor doesn't come out until they get into hot water. That tickles me.*

### INGREDIENTS

mint tea leaves
**4** quarts water
**1** quart sugar

### INSTRUCTIONS

Fill 1 quart jar with meadow (fuzzy mint) tea leaves. Pack tightly. Bring water to boil and add tea leaves. Allow to steep 15 minutes, tightly covered. Remove leaves and add sugar. Stir well and freeze. Use 1 quart concentrate to 3 quarts of water.

# Real Lemonade

**Makes 3 quarts**

### INGREDIENTS

**6** lemons
**1½** cup sugar
**2½** quarts cold water

### INSTRUCTIONS

Squeeze lemons and add sugar. Or, thinly slice the lemons (unpeeled), add sugar, and mash with a potato masher. Mix very well before adding water.

# Cherry Punch

**Makes about 4 quarts**

### INGREDIENTS

- **2** packages cherry powdered drink mix
- **2** cups sugar
- **3** quarts water
- **1** (6-ounce) can frozen orange juice concentrate
- **1** (6-ounce) can frozen lemon juice concentrate
- **1** quart ginger ale

### INSTRUCTIONS

Mix all ingredients together. Pour some into ice cube trays to use to chill the drink.

# Orange Sherbet Punch

**Makes 5 quarts**

### INGREDIENTS

- **1** package orange powdered drink mix
- **1** cup sugar
- **2** quarts water
- **2** quarts lemon-lime soda
- **1** quart orange soda
- **1** quart orange sherbet

### INSTRUCTIONS

Mix and serve.

# Chocolate Syrup

**Makes 1 gallon chocolate milk**

*One dark Saturday night, our neighbors' shed burned to the ground. Many friends and neighbors brought food and helped clean up and rebuild. One woman gave cocoa and this recipe. It was new to me, and we all loved it. We now use it at our house because it saves money, as we buy cocoa in bulk.*

### INGREDIENTS

**1½–2** cups sugar

**1** cup unsweetened cocoa powder

**⅓** teaspoon salt

**1⅓** cup hot water

**1** tablespoon vanilla

### INSTRUCTIONS

Mix sugar, cocoa, salt, and hot water. Boil 3 minutes. Cool. Add vanilla. Pour into jar and store in refrigerator. Use for chocolate milk or wherever you use chocolate syrup.

# Fresh Fruit Milkshake

**Serves 1–2**

*This is very good on a hot summer day when you come in from gardening, working in the fields, or playing.*

### INGREDIENTS

**½** cup fresh strawberries (or peaches, raspberries, or blueberries)

**1½** cup vanilla ice cream

**¾** cup cold milk

### INSTRUCTIONS

Wash and mash the fruit. Add ice cream and milk and beat until frothy. Serve.

# Rhubarb Drink

**Makes about 8 quarts**

*This was a new recipe for our family last spring. Mom made 210 quarts, and by the middle of August, it was all gone! When we mowed the yard, we got hot and thirsty, and that's what we went for. When Dad and the boys were making hay, rhubarb drink is what they asked for, too. So be sure and try this delicious summertime drink!*

### INGREDIENTS

- **4** pounds rhubarb
- **4** quarts water
- **2** cups sugar
- **1** cup pineapple juice
- **1** (6-ounce) can frozen orange juice concentrate

### INSTRUCTIONS

Boil rhubarb and water together until rhubarb is soft. Strain or puree and add the remaining ingredients in order given. Pour into jars, seal, and process in boiling water bath for 10 minutes according to your canner's directions.

# Amish Church Spread

**Makes 2 gallons**

*We like if there is leftover Church Spread. We put a generous amount of Church Spread on a ½-inch thick slice of homemade bread. Put a sliced pineapple ring on top, then add a scoop of home-made vanilla ice cream. Eat with a spoon as dessert.*

### INGREDIENTS

- **1** gallon King Syrup molasses
- **1** gallon marshmallow crème
- **4** cups smooth peanut butter

### INSTRUCTIONS

Mix together well. Store in refrigerator.

# Kitchen-Made Apple Butter

**Makes about 24 pints**

## INGREDIENTS

**4** gallons apples, cored and chopped but not peeled

**8** pounds white sugar

**1** quart good apple cider

**2** teaspoons cinnamon, or to taste

## INSTRUCTIONS

Place apples and sugar in large kettle and let stand overnight. The next morning, add apple cider, which improves the flavor a lot. Cook, covered, slowly on range or oil stove for at least 3 hours. Drain off juice and work pulp through colander to get all the juice out of it. Cook juice until it gels. Add cinnamon and cook a while longer. Can while still hot according to your canner's directions.

# Rosy Rhubarb Preserves

**Makes about 4 pints**

*One summer evening after supper, I was making a batch of rhubarb preserves. I had added the sugar and was stirring it when the sky became dark and stormy and thunder rumbled in the west. Big drops of rain began to fall, and I quickly ran upstairs to close the windows. Suddenly there was a sharp crack of thunder and the electricity went off. The wind was lashing the trees and the top of our pear tree broke off and crashed down. At bedtime, the electricity still hadn't come back on, and we were worried the food in the refrigerator would spoil. At eleven o'clock we were awakened by the smoke detector and hurried to the kitchen. The electricity had come back on and my rhubarb preserves boiled until they scorched and activated the smoke detector. I had forgotten to turn off the burner under the kettle!*

## INGREDIENTS

**5** cups rhubarb, cut fine

**1** cup crushed pineapple, drained

**4** cups sugar

**½** cup strawberry gelatin

## INSTRUCTIONS

Combine rhubarb, pineapple, and sugar in a kettle. Place over low heat and stir gently until sugar is dissolved. Cook over medium heat until mixture becomes clear—about 10–12 minutes. Remove from heat and add gelatin. Pour into jars and seal according to your canner's directions.

# Strawberry Jam

**Makes about 12 half-pints**

*Once when I was making strawberry jam to can, I was just stirring in the Therm-flo when my little daughter cried, "Mam, come look, the birdies are hatched, the birdies are hatched! Oh! Just look!" There was a nest under the porch eaves. I thought I'd join her at the window for just a moment, but I got caught up in the excitement and forgot the strawberry jam. It scorched a bit at the bottom. That winter, every time we opened a jar of the jam and tasted the slight scorch, we thought of the little robins and wondered where they were now—maybe down in the sunny South, enjoying summerlike weather.*

## INGREDIENTS

**1** quart water

**1** cup sugar

**1** package strawberry powdered drink mix

**½** cup Clear Jel

**2** quarts strawberries

## INSTRUCTIONS

Bring water, sugar, and powdered drink mix to a boil. Thicken with ½ cup Clear Jel mixed with a little water. Remove from heat. Wash, cap, and halve the berries. When sugar mixture is cold, add the berries to it. Can according to your canner's directions.

# Mock Raspberry Jam

**Makes about 7 cups**

## INGREDIENTS

**5** cups green tomatoes, ground

**4** cups sugar

**1** (6-ounce) box raspberry gelatin

## INSTRUCTIONS

Bring ingredients to a full rolling boil. Boil 20 minutes for thick jam, less for thinner jam. Keep stirring. Turn off heat. Add gelatin. Stir until dissolved. Place in jars and can according to your canner's directions.

# Ellen's Soda Cheese

**Makes about 1 quart**

We've always had a cow or two, with plenty of extra milk for making cheese and butter. Mom was most always too busy with her other duties, so the cheese making fell to us girls. Dad liked his home-made cheese, and so when I was fourteen years old, he got me interested in making it. My older sister (our regular cheese maker) had gotten married that year and moved far away, and I wished I had asked her more about it before I attempted it myself.

I had beginner's luck, though, and the first time it turned out just right! But to my humiliation, the next batch was a flop, and we had to feed it to the pigs! I got teased a lot by my older brothers about that, and still do sometimes at our family gatherings.

It's really not that hard once you get a little experience (which I should have by now, for I've been making it for over twenty years). I'd encourage anyone who has a cow or extra milk to try it. With the sky-high price of cheese at the grocery stores, it sure is a savings.

## INGREDIENTS

- **1** gallon sour milk
- **½** teaspoon baking soda
- **3** tablespoons butter
- **1** cup cream
- **1** teaspoon salt
- **1** egg, beaten

## INSTRUCTIONS

Heat sour milk to 115°. Cut through both ways with a knife to aid heating. Pour into a cloth bag and hang overnight to drain thoroughly. When dry, crumble and stir in baking soda and butter. Let stand 5 hours. Place in double boiler and allow to melt. Add cream and stir until smooth. Add salt and egg. Boil 3 minutes, or until egg is cooked. Pour into a dish.

## Lucy's Kitchen Tip

On winter washdays, rub vinegar over your hands and dry them thoroughly just before hanging out the wash. This keeps hands from getting so cold. Have the clothes-pins good and warm, too.

# Salt Substitute

*Season foods with herbs and spices if you're on a low-salt diet. I still use salt, but this is an excellent substitute to bring out more flavor in soups, vegetables, etc.*

## INGREDIENTS

- **1** teaspoon chili powder
- **1** tablespoon garlic powder
- **6** tablespoons onion powder
- **1** teaspoon oregano
- **3** tablespoons paprika
- **2** tablespoons pepper
- **1** tablespoon poultry seasoning
- **2** tablespoons dry mustard

## INSTRUCTIONS

Combine all ingredients, mixing well. Place in salt shaker and use instead of salt.

# Pantry Plant Food

## INGREDIENTS

- **1** teaspoon baking powder
- **1** teaspoon Epsom salts
- **1** teaspoon saltpeter
- **½** teaspoon household ammonia

## INSTRUCTIONS

Mix with 1 gallon lukewarm water. Give this to plants in place of a regular watering once a month. This gives houseplants a boost, especially vines and ivies.

# Bird Treats

One day this summer, Dad found a baby bird. We thought it had likely fallen down while trying to learn to fly.

We kept it in a box with hopes of taking care of it until it could fly. Later we found a second bird, and now there were two hungry mouths to feed. They made enough noise that we knew they wanted something. When they opened their mouths, it was surprising how big they actually were.

We thought we could fill those hungry mouths at least as good as a mother bird. We took the fly swatter and went through the kitchen and porch in search of flies to feed them. We also dug worms for them.

Once we decided to see what our hen with three chicks would say about another "baby." She quickly put an end to that idea! She flew at that tiny bird so angrily that we were afraid she'd kill it before we could get it away.

## INGREDIENTS

**1** cup suet or lard, melted

**1** cup peanut butter

**1** cup cornmeal

**1** cup oatmeal

**¼** cup sugar

## INSTRUCTIONS

Mix all together; add sunflower seeds and other bird seed in amounts desired. Serve on birdfeeder.

# Homemade Baby Wipes

*We had been a childless couple for a number of years. So of course our first little girl brought much joy. Then my sister shared this recipe with me, and I really like it. Wipes are so handy with a little one in the house. Now our little girl will soon be four years old, and we don't know if there will be any more of these precious little ones for us. But we are so thankful we were blessed with at least one. She certainly has been a joy for us.*

## INGREDIENTS

- **1** roll paper towels, cut in half
- **2½** cups water
- **2** tablespoons liquid baby wash
- **2** tablespoons baby oil
- **1** (10-cup) plastic bowl with lid

## INSTRUCTIONS

Put a half roll of paper towels in bowl; in a separate bowl, mix the rest of ingredients. Pour liquid over towels. To start, pull wipes out of the middle of roll. Drill or melt a hole in middle of lid and pull wipes out through hole.

# Amazing Cleaner

## INGREDIENTS

- **1** cup ammonia
- **½** cup vinegar
- **¼** cup baking soda
- **1** gallon water

## INSTRUCTIONS

Mix all together. Good for washing walls and for tough jobs.

# Food to Prepare for a Barn Raising

## Enough food to feed 180 men

I've attended quite a few barn raisings in my time and helped to get a hearty meal to the table for the hungry, hard-working men. It sure is amazing how much can be accomplished in one day if so many willing workers get together and roll up their sleeves. We're always happy when the work is done and thankful if no one gets hurt.

When I was five years old, our neighbor's barn was struck by lightning and burned down. At the barn raising, we children were playing a game and I collided with another child and my two front teeth were knocked out. I couldn't eat sweet corn off the cob that summer, but by the next summer, I had grown another set.

The next barn raising I attended was at my uncle's place—tornado-like winds had blown down their shed. Daddy used to remind us that we should always be willing to drop our own work to help others, for we never know how soon we will be the ones who need the help.

## MENU

| | |
|---|---|
| **50** | pounds white potatoes |
| **30** | pounds sweet potatoes |
| **20** | plump chickens |
| **50** | pounds roast beef |
| **3** | hams |
| **15** | large loaves of bread |
| **300** | yeast rolls |
| **2** | gallons cucumber pickles |
| **10** | dozen red beet eggs |
| **120** | shoofly pies |
| **500** | lard cakes (doughnuts) |
| **1** | dozen sponge cakes |
| **15** | quarts applesauce |
| **3** | gallons soft custard |
| **4** | gallons rice pudding |
| **1** | large crock stewed prunes |
| **5** | gallon stone jar lemonade |
| **5** | gallon stone jar meadow tea |

# *Index*

# About the Compiler

Lucy Leid is an Old Order Mennonite cook, wife, and mother who lives in Lancaster County, Pennsylvania. She and her husband grow wholesale nursery stock on a small evergreen farm. As members of the Groffdale Conference, Leid and her family use horse-and-buggy transportation and wear plain dress.